SMALL TOWNS, DARK SECRETS

SOCIAL MEDIA, REALITY TV AND MURDER IN
RURAL AMERICA

EILEEN ORMSBY

WHAT CRITICS HAVE SAID ABOUT EILEEN ORMSBY'S BOOKS

"Ormsby has delivered a triumph of narrative journalism, meticulously researched and gripping, a skilful mergence of tech jargon with human drama." *The Saturday Paper*

"The book is a fascinating expose of this particular aspect of the "dark web" of internet dealings and its subsequent unravelling." *Sydney Morning Herald*

"Ormsby's investigative journalism shines as she provides a very thorough account of Ulbricht's rise and fall." *Penthouse Magazine*

"What pulls you through The Darkest Web isn't its often-nefarious, sometimes-gory details, but Ormsby's handling of three progressively intense narrative arcs." *The Guardian*

"The darknet has become a repository for human cruelty, perversion and psychosis, and Ormsby captures all the tragedy in her gripping book." *The Australian*

"A great strength of the meticulously researched Silk Road is the manner in which Ormsby gently takes the reader by the hand, unpacking the technology underpinning this 'dark net' market." *Australian Police Journal*

"A disillusioned corporate lawyer turned writer from Australia, Eileen's new book, The Darkest Web, is the story of her journey, from drug markets and contract killing sites to the Internet's seediest alcoves. But the most startling moments of the book happen when she comes face-to-face with some of its key players." *VICE*

"From the Internet's hidden drug dens to torture-porn websites, Ormsby has seen it all. If you've ever wondered what the Dark Web is really like, Darkest Web should be on your TBR." *Bustle Magazine: The Best New True Crime Books You Can Read Right Now*

"Riveting." *Who Magazine*

"Investigative journalism that gallops along at a cracking pace." *SMH Good Weekend*

"Through her clear rendering of the facts, Ormsby makes the intricacies of the technology involved accessible to even the most technophobic of readers. The tone is conversational and friendly while the content is intriguing and increasingly dark. In her quest to uncover the mystery behind the enigmatic DPR she uncovers a story of subterfuge, replete with conspiracy theories and hidden identities, that is rich with anecdotes." *Newtown Review of Books*

"Ormsby is a great writer, giving us gripping accounts from the people who actually used "Silk Road" to paint an accurate picture of how the website was created, run, and ultimately fell . . . Silk Road is easily one of the best books I've read this year." *The Library NZ*

"Silk Road is one of the more readable and gripping true crime books of recent times. It is not just Ormsby's knowledge of the brief but spectacular rise and fall of Silk Road that makes for compelling reading, but also the ordering of the material so that the reader has the sense of being educated in the technical and legal background to an astonishing criminal enterprise." *The Australian*

"For the most complete account of the original Silk Road ... Eileen Ormsby's book Silk Road is the best place to start. It's full of original research, interviews and insight. This is best read along with her excellent blog, AllThingsVice, which covers several aspects of the dark net, but especially the dark net markets." *Jamie Bartlett, author of Darknet and Radicals*

"[*Stalkers* is] chilling... harrowing...unpicks the sordid tale from the start" *The Sun*

"Dark, disturbing and near unbelievable... [*Stalkers* is] my No.1 true crime read this year" *OzNoir*

ABOUT THE AUTHOR

Eileen Ormsby is a lawyer, author and freelance journalist based in Melbourne. Her first book, "Silk Road" was the world's first in-depth expose of the black markets that operate on the dark web. In "The Darkest Web", Eileen's gonzo-style investigations led her deep into the secretive corners of the dark web where drugs and weapons dealers, hackers, hitmen and worse ply their trade. Many of these dark web interactions turned into real-world relationships, entanglements, hack attempts on her computer and even death threats from the dark web's most successful hitman network.

Eileen started writing scripts for the Casefile True Crime Podcast in 2018 and has since become one of their most regular contributors. She often focuses on cases that have a dark web or internet aspect to them.

BOOKS BY EILEEN ORMSBY

A Manual for Murder: FREE AND EXCLUSIVE

Psycho.com: serial killers on the internet

Murder on the Dark Web: true stories from the dark side of the internet

Stalkers: true tales of deadly obsessions

Little Girls Lost: true tales of heinous crimes

Mishap or Murder? True tales of mysterious deaths and disappearances

The Darkest Web

Silk Road

Sneak peeks of these books and a link to your FREE TRUE CRIME BOOK are in the back matter

INTRODUCTION

In the United States, nearly one fifth of the population - around 58 million people - live in rural areas, and most of those live in small towns. Some grew up there and stayed, continuing the lifestyle enjoyed by the generations before them; others made the move to escape the hustle and bustle of urban life, or to provide a safe, wholesome way of living for their children.

Of course, not all small towns in America are the same. Some are known as hippie havens, others are home to wealthy executives. There are mountain towns in the southeast, desert towns in the southwest, communities nestled in dense forests of northern midwest, and thousands more, each with their own specific economic and cultural characteristics.

In the last decade, several small towns in the United States have seen more businesses closing than opening, and the population has declined as a result. Some of the most severely affected are the towns in the so-called Bible Belt. Such towns are often characterized by a high unemployment rate, the lack of activities for young people, and the cultural, political, religious, and economic influence of evangelical Christianity. The Baptist church on the end of the street and the Presbyterian church at the center of town don't just preach morality and salvation on Sunday. They meet with local politicians to discuss state budgets. They teach Sunday school classes for children and Bible study for adults. In many such communities, there is nothing for young people to do but work hard, play in the local band, and get married right out of high school. Then they have kids and buy a house and never move again.

These are often homogenous communities and some contend that rural America has become a war-zone of sectarian and ethnic groups, paranoid of each other, quick to take offense and quicker to take up arms. Many long-term residents don't like outsiders. People are tense and polite, but unwelcoming and hostile to strangers. But despite the apparently simple facade, many of these small towns are complex and layered places filled with secrets

This book looks at two recent cases where the vagaries of small town living led to multiple unexpected and shocking murders.

It is not surprising that isolated young people with not much to do turn to social media. But their interactions can become toxic, anything but friendly. When everybody already knows everyone else's business, online arguments, where the participants might be anonymous, can become enormous. This was the case in the double murder of Bill Payne and Billie Jean Hayworth, which was rumored to have come about because the victims unfriended someone else on Facebook. Investigators soon discovered a feud that had been simmering in full view of the entire town of Mountain City for over a year.

At the other end of the scale the Stockdale Family was

private and insular, the children homeschooled, their only outlet playing in the family Bluegrass band. The internet and television were banned, movies and radio programs vetted to ensure they adhered to the family's fundamentalist Christian values. They kept to themselves on their farm in Ohio, until an unexpected call from the producers of reality TV series Wife Swap upended their world. Was it the scrutiny of a skeptical public that led to the tragic circumstances some years later?

Mountain City, Tennessee and Bolivar, Ohio: just two small towns that harbored dark secrets.

UNFRIENDLY

HOW A SOCIAL MEDIA FEUD LED TO A DOUBLE HOMICIDE

Note: The spelling and punctuation of some emails and social media posts have been cleaned up for the sake of readability. This does not affect the meaning or intent of the messages. For the sake of transparency, the full, unedited versions of key emails and social media posts are in the appendix. All spelling, grammar and punctuation errors in quoted extracts are those of the authors of those emails and posts.

WELCOME TO MOUNTAIN CITY

Mountain City, Johnson County - if you can't see the mountains from your front porch, then you might not even be in the right town. Nestled in the north-eastern corner of Tennessee, it's one of those towns that people describe as "sleepy" or "slow-paced." With a cost of living almost 30 per cent lower than the national average, taking it easy is a popular pastime in Mountain City. The summers are warm, the winters short, cold and wet, and it's at least partly cloudy year-round. Most people own a gun. Many own several. There is no public transit, so everybody has a car, and that car is more often than not a pickup truck with a bull bar on the front and, a gun rack on the back and spare magazines in the glove compartment.

To get to Mountain City, you take the scenic route along Highway 421, which runs alongside Watauga Lake. Often referred to as "The Snake" by motor enthusiasts and cyclists, locals will warn you that the highway's curves and sharp drop-offs are not for the faint-hearted. On approach, a sign greets visitors:

Welcome to Mountain City
A friendly hometown

The town is home to antique, outlet, and thrift stores, churches, several dining options, a library, a community theater, a hospital, three grocery stores, a fitness center, a vineyard and winery, hiking trails, and beloved fishing and hunting spots. But, although it might have its charms, Mountain City is far from idyllic.

In 2012, a lack of education, high rates of poverty, and rampant drug use characterized the town. Due to the prevalence of low-wage jobs and unemployment, the average citizen of Mountain City earned about half as much as the average Tennessean. Around thirty-five per cent of Mountain City residents lived below the poverty line, and many struggled to find work thanks to a local unemployment rate far higher than the national average. Both the manufacture and use of methamphetamine were prevalent. Politically it was staunchly conservative, a Republican stronghold, with the Democrats rarely garnering fifteen per cent of the vote. Its homogenous population mostly described themselves as Christian, but many acted in decidedly un-Christianlike ways. God, guns and country, but not necessarily in that order. Less charitable observers characterized the town as "redneck" or "hillbilly."

The scenery was stunning, and the cost of living was cheap. But there was a reason for that. As one person wrote on a local news site: "That's because the demand for living here ain't too high ... everything from jobs, education, and just life around here needs to catch up."

Despite all of this, Mountain City's rate of violent crime —homicides and assaults—was consistently below that of

Tennessee's major cities, Memphis and Nashville, as well as most towns of comparable size, every year.

Every year, that is, except 2012. In 2012, violent crime spiked, shooting above both the state and national average.

With around 2,500 residents spread out over an area of 3.3 square miles, people tended to know one another's business and small feuds could easily fester and spread, neighbors taking sides depending on friendships, gossip, and for lack of anything better to do. Later, people said they could trace the horror that unfolded in 2012 back to social media, and in particular one incident: someone unfriended someone else on Facebook.

The truth is a little more complicated.

Actually, the truth is a LOT more complicated.

A GRISLY DISCOVERY

A t around 6:30 a.m., on the morning of January 31, 2012, Brad Osborne made his usual drive to pick up his friend and co-worker, Bill Clay Payne and take him to work. The two men worked at Parkdale Mills, a textile plant in their hometown of Mountain City, and often carpooled. As well as being work colleagues, they were friends, and Brad sometimes stayed with Bill when having marital issues with his wife, Tara.

Bill lived in his father's white, single-story clapboard house on James Davis Lane, so close to Highway 67 that a stone stirred up by a speeding truck could land in the front yard. Bill lived there with his partner, Billie Jean Hayworth, their baby son, Tyler, and his father, Billy Ray Payne, who was better known around town as "Paw Bill." Paw Bill was a laid-back, soft-spoken man, with shaggy blond hair and a matching beard who was devoted to, and proud of, his kids. It surprised nobody that he let his son and his fiancée live with him as they found their feet as a new family. As one friend put it, "If everyone was as easygoing as him, the world would be a much nicer place." Paw Bill never missed an opportunity to whip out his phone and show his workmates new photos of his kids or grandkids. Many suspected he secretly hoped that Bill, Billie Jean, and their baby wouldn't ever move out.

When Brad Osborne arrived that morning, Paw Bill had already left about an hour earlier, for his job at the IRC manufacturing plant where he had worked for nearly forty years. The plant was located over the border, in Boone, North Carolina, about thirty-five minutes away. Billie Jean's car was in the driveway, underneath the double carport as usual, but Bill's was not. Brad pulled up and left his car idling, as he did every morning. Usually, Bill came right out as soon as Brad arrived. They started work at 7 a.m., but the drive wasn't far, so there was plenty of time to cover any unexpected minor delays. The sun had yet to rise, so he could clearly see that the light was on in Bill's bedroom window, though there was no sign of any movement. Brad tooted the horn and waited for his friend to emerge.

As the minutes ticked by, Brad became increasingly concerned about being late for work, even though the plant was only a few minutes' drive. Not wanting to leave the warmth of his car, Brad tried calling Bill's cell phone, but he didn't answer. After receiving no response to another blast of his horn, Brad decided to brave the cold, wintery morning and hurry his friend along.

Knowing that the rear sliding glass door was rarely locked, Brad made his way down the side of the house and let himself in after knocking once, calling out Bill's name several times. He could hear the shrill beeping of an alarm clock coming from one bedroom. Brad picked up the land-line in the living room and tried calling Bill's cell phone again, but he didn't hear it ringing inside the house. He thought he heard the quiet whimper of a baby, but he wasn't sure. Not feeling comfortable entering the bedrooms where Billie Jean and her baby might be sleeping, Brad tried calling out once more before going back out the way he came, the incessant beeping of the alarm fading as he closed the door behind him. Confused, he drove to work on his own. Bill was not at the plant when he arrived and did not turn up as the morning wore on. It was certainly out of character, but Brad assumed there must be a logical explanation.

Later that morning, at around 10:00 a.m., Paw Bill's former neighbor, Roy Stephens, and his wife Linda pulled into the driveway. Roy and Linda had an on again/off again relationship, and they were there to pick up Roy's mail, which he was having forwarded to Paw Bill's place while he and Linda tried to sort through their marital problems. It was easier to have one location to collect it from rather than having it follow him as he moved from place to place. Linda stayed in the car while Roy took the same path Brad Osborne had taken a few hours earlier. Assuming that Billie Jean was home, as her car was in the driveway, Roy knocked on the sliding glass door before letting himself in. Whoever brought in the mail placed it on a shelf in the living room so that Roy could come and get it whenever he wanted.

Roy knew the house well, as Paw Bill sometimes let him stay on the couch when he was fighting with Linda. Taking the mail, Roy hollered out, sure that somebody must be home. Receiving no response, he continued to call out as he ventured down the hallway, toward where he knew the bedrooms were. As he approached the first room, he saw a trail of what looked like blood near the doorway. The moment he looked inside, it was very clear where the blood had come from.

Bill Payne laid motionless on his back on the bed, face bruised and blackened and blood from a bullet wound coagulating around his neck. He was naked, except for his boxer shorts, looking as though the intruder had surprised him while he was getting dressed for work. Roy sprang toward him, grabbed him by the arms, and shook him, hoping to get some sort of response. When he got none, he raced out of the house to the car, yelling for Linda to come to his aid.

Linda, who was trained in CPR, rushed into the house and to the bedroom, hoping her skills could revive their friend. It didn't take long for her to realize that it was futile. When she tried to find a pulse in Bill's neck, he was stiff and ice-cold, and she saw he had a gash across his throat, in addition to the bullet wound. Linda used the cordless phone in the living room to dial 911.

As Linda nervously waited for the operator, Roy thought he heard something coming from another part of the house. Not sure what to expect, he made his way down the hallway to a second bedroom, following a trail of bloody dog paw prints that led to Paw Bill's Jack Russell, Pepper, who appeared unharmed. However, what greeted Roy in the second bedroom was worse than anything he could have ever imagined.

23-year-old Billie Jean Hayworth lay on the floor of what appeared to be a nursery, looking every bit as deceased as her partner. She was wearing Christmas Grinch pajamas and a pool of blood surrounded her head, with fragments of dark brown hair and skin on the carpet next to her. Roy didn't need to touch her to know that he would find no pulse.

It was the child in her arms who had made the noise.

Seven-month-old Tyler Payne was still being held tightly by his lifeless mother. He had blood on his sleeper suit and on the back of his head. Lying beside the pair was a small Snoopy doll, as though Billie Jean had been holding it to comfort her infant son. Next to them was a Pack-n-Play multi-use playpen, with a full bottle of formula lying inside, out of reach of the hungry baby.

Roy barely dared approach, but he had to know. Relief flooded through him when he realized the baby was breathing. Tyler appeared to be physically unharmed, and was merely in a deep sleep, although the red blotches on his face suggested he had recently been crying. All the blood belonged to his mother, who continued to grip the baby tightly, as though still protecting him, even in death. Roy yelled out to his wife to alert her to what he had found, and she rushed into the room to see the baby, now being held safely in Roy's arms, for herself.

"I need an ambulance, fast!" she gasped into the phone when the 911 operator responded. "There's no pulse. There's no pulse on either one of them ... there's a baby involved. The baby's here ... Bill Payne's not responsive ... he's in one room, she's in the other, by the playpen. It kind of looks like she was trying to get to her baby."

"Do you know how long they've been there?" asked the operator.

"I don't know. They're cold. They're white." Linda somehow held it together as she provided as much information as she could to the operator, but her voice disintegrated when she spoke of little Tyler. "The baby, kind of to me ... as a parent ... looks like maybe it's been crying for a while, and probably cried 'til he couldn't cry no more," she sobbed.

3

INVESTIGATION AND ARREST

I t didn't take long for Johnson County Rescue to arrive at the scene. Paramedics checked Bill and Billie Jean over and confirmed what was painfully obvious to Roy and Linda Stephens; the young couple was dead, but their baby son appeared to be unharmed. Johnson County Sheriff Mike Reece, accompanied by local police officers, arrived soon after the medics and secured the scene. Roy explained he had not touched the bodies, but had instinctively grabbed Tyler from his mother's arms when he realized the baby was breathing.

Later, an autopsy of Bill and Billie determined that both victims had been shot in the head, and that Bill also suffered deep slash wounds to his neck, although it was unclear whether that had occurred before or after death. Neither of them had any defensive wounds, suggesting they had been taken by surprise. After ruling out the possibility of a murder-suicide, the deaths were declared homicides by a person or persons unknown.

The time frame for when the young couple had been killed was narrow. Everything was normal when Paw Bill had left for work at around 5:30 that morning, and they were presumably dead by the time Brad Osborne arrived to pick up Bill an hour later. Had the killer known the household's morning routine, waiting for Paw Bill to leave before embarking on their deadly rampage?

Tennessee Bureau of Investigation (TBI) Agent Scott Lott arrived on the scene later that morning. Like nearly every home in the county, there were several guns at the residence, but the shotguns and .22 caliber pistol he located were not the weapons that been used to kill Bill and Billie Jean. The bullets, which had traveled right through the heads of the victims, one lodging in Bill's pillow and the other in the baby's bouncy seat, had come from a .38 caliber or 9mm handgun. There were no spent casings, suggesting the shooter had used a revolver, or taken the time to collect them.

Neighbors Bruce and Marilyn Beeding, who described the pair as a nice young couple, had heard nothing unusual in the early hours of the morning. Usually Paw Bill's dog, Pepper, barked if any strangers came to the house, which made the investigators wonder if the killer was someone known to the family. Had the victims perhaps even welcomed them into the house?

As police and medics swarmed and secured the house, child protective services took baby Tyler to the local hospital for examination, where he would be held until they could determine the most appropriate family members for him to be released to.

After ruling out domestic violence or murder-suicide, the next most likely explanation was a drug deal that had not gone to plan. A search of the house revealed a small quantity of drugs, including methamphetamine still sitting out on a plate, with a straw beside it, as if ready to be snorted, in the nursery. Police also recovered a meth pipe, and some prescription medication. Such findings were not completely unexpected, considering the demographic of Mountain City, but nobody in the household was on the police radar as being involved in drug activity.

Investigators quickly contacted as many of the couple's close friends as they could. The sheriff's initial enquiries centered on Bill's missing car, but once located they established he had loaned it out some time ago and so it being missing had no bearing on the investigation.

Billie Jean's best friend, Lindsey Thomas, made a statement to police that she had been at the house the day before and that Billie Jean had told her she had received a fresh batch of pills for her and Bill to sell. The couple apparently took part in low-level drug dealing to make a little extra cash and to buy things for the baby. Lindsey wondered if Bill had planned to meet with someone before he left for work and whether the murders were indeed the result of a drug deal gone bad.

Bill's cell phone records showed two telephone numbers had called Bill late the prior evening. Those numbers led to two of Bill's friends, who, upon discovering the police's motivation to speak to them, readily admitted that they occasionally bought pills from Bill. It was certainly no major drug operation; Bill simply sold or swapped his Suboxone among a small group of contacts. His friends claimed they had intended to pick up some Suboxone strips from Bill that evening, but he had sent a text message at 11:30 p.m. saying that he was tired and would not meet them.

Agent Lott welcomed the candor of the couple's friends and believed the two men who had hoped to purchase drugs were being honest with him. If it wasn't a drug deal gone bad, they needed to look for other motives. Mountain City was a small town where everyone knew everyone else's business. Investigators already felt that an arrest would not be far away.

The day after the murders, police interviewed Bill Payne's cousin, Jamie Curd. Several people had mentioned that the two had once been close, but had recently fallen out. Jamie explained that this was because Bill had been ranting about something that was posted on Facebook. Jamie didn't have a Facebook account and denied knowing anything about the killings, but something about his demeanor kept him high on the police's list of suspects.

Later that week, after several other leads and interviews with various residents of the close-knit town, the police brought Jamie back into the station and asked him to take a polygraph test. He was nervous, and the test indicated he lied in response to several questions but, most notably, it appeared that he lied about knowing the identity of the couple's killer. Polygraphs are notoriously unreliable and the results not admissible in court, but they can be an effective intimidation tactic. The police set about interrogating Bill's cousin in the claustrophobic little office that doubled as an interview room. Part way through the intense grilling, Jamie surprised his interrogators with a question that seemed to come out of left field. "Is the CIA here?"

The question mystified the police. "Why did you ask about the CIA?"

"Because he says he works for them," Jamie replied.

When they probed a little more, Jamie Curd told detectives he'd been working with a man named Chris who was in the CIA and that it was Chris's job to protect one of the other citizens of Mountain City, at all costs. Her name was Jenelle Potter.

4

MEET THE POTTERS

Most everyone knows me in some way or another. I'm a very sweet, caring person. I'm from Kennett Sq PA but I have been living in East Tennessee for going on 9 years ... I love life and I love to make others laugh. I'm fun and caring and loving and sweet. If anyone needs anything they let me know. I love to make new friends or talk to just about anyone. I love my Family so much. My Mom and Dad are my world. I do not party or drink or smoke at all. Thank you for reading this

— JENELLE POTTER'S FACEBOOK
INTRODUCTION

The Potter family, comprising patriarch Marvin, his wife Barbara and their adult daughter Jenelle, lived in a nondescript three-bedroom house on Hospital Road, a little over five miles from Paw Bill's. They were not lifetime residents of the town, having moved there eight years earlier, in 2004. They had previously lived in Pennsylvania, about forty minutes west of Philadelphia, with their elder daughter, Christie.

Marvin Potter, better known as Buddy, was a veteran, and he was proud of that fact. He often regaled his family with tales of his time in the Marines, boasting of the time when he served in the Vietnam War and assisted his fellow injured Marines to safety. Those actions earned him the Navy Cross Medal, the second-highest military award for valor. He added it to his collection of three Silver Stars (the third-highest valor award), Bronze Star (fourth highest), Purple Heart, Airborne Wings, and SCUBA badges. Photographs of himself wearing his uniform with the medals, badges, and decorations adorned his walls. He told anyone who would listen about his three tours in 'Nam, including some time spent in the Briar Patch POW camp. After attending jump, diving, survival, and recon schools, he had been assigned to Marine Force Reconnaissance, a special operations force tasked with military intelligence missions. It was then, he said, that he began working with the CIA, but everything that happened after that was classified and he couldn't talk about it to anybody.

Buddy's career came to an abrupt halt when he had an accident while working on high tension electric poles. From then on, Buddy had been on disability. There were many times in Jenelle and Christie's childhood that Buddy was in so much pain that he could not get out of a chair. He also had pulmonary issues and often walked with a cane. He needed supplemental oxygen, and the tanks soon became a permanent feature of the house, sometimes doubling as stands for rounds of ammo. Buddy was a big believer in guns, and the Potters spent many of their family outings at the gun range. Stickers covering the back windshield of Buddy's truck left no doubt that this was a family that staunchly supported the Second Amendment, as well as the NRA.

Christie's childhood was relatively normal, but her little sister Jenelle received the bulk of their parents' attention. Born in 1982, Jenelle had a slew of health problems, including Type 1 diabetes and partial deafness. When she was a child, her parents tried many approaches to fix her auditory disability, and they placed her into speech therapy. However, Jenelle faced significant learning difficulties. Her IQ of 72 meant she never operated beyond a fourth-grade level. She spent her entire school life in Special Ed. By the time Jenelle graduated from high school, she could read and write, but didn't have the skills to get, or hold, a job.

Because of her profound difficulties, Jenelle's reasoning and interaction with other people had always been a little odd. Jenelle could not read social cues and did not understand when other kids were joking, making her takethings more seriously than she should. As a result, she had trouble making friends, and often got into disagreements and conflicts. When she did, her parents stepped in to smooth things over or threaten the other party until they backed down. In one instance, during middle school, a dispute between Jenelle and another girl almost escalated to the courtroom. Jenelle claimed the girl had punched her, fuelled by jealousy because Jenelle was "too pretty."

Christie noted her parents coddled her little sister, always taking care of any issues she faced, including those that were of her own making. Jenelle sometimes sought attention by malingering, occasionally claiming she had cancer, or collapsing dramatically in the hallways, waiting for people to notice and make a fuss over her.

Jenelle's parents tried to make her fit in at Kennett High School in Pennsylvania, but they also drummed into her how different she was, gushing that this made her special and better than the other kids. These mixed messages made

Jenelle confused and unable to function socially with her peers. As soon as she graduated, Jenelle received social security and disability, and lived at home with her parents, who took care of all her needs.

Jenelle was a tall and gangly teenager. By the time she was an adult, she stood at over six feet, towering over the other girls as well as most of the boys. She had the misfortune of a high-pitched, childish voice that was incongruous with her large frame. This decidedly peculiar juxtaposition didn't help her social awkwardness.

It wasn't only her schoolmates that Jenelle didn't get along with—she hated her sister as well. Over time, Christie came to believe that her little sister's disabilities were "not as bad as everybody else said they were." She felt Jenelle manipulated and deceived other people for her own ends, especially their parents. Christie felt herself being pushed more and more to the sidelines as her parents became even more consumed by loving and protecting their favored daughter, Jenelle.

5

THE POTTERS MOVE TO MOUNTAIN CITY

I would like to meet Jessica Simpson and I would love to meet President Bush. I would like to meet the cast of "Gilmore Girls," and I would love to meet a SWAT team from a big city.

— JENELLE POTTER'S MYSPACE PAGE

I n 2004, when Jenelle was 23 years old, Buddy, Barbara, and Jenelle moved to Mountain City. Christie did not go with them, having moved out of home five years earlier, and having had little to do with her family since. Her parents not only didn't mind the estrangement from their older daughter, they seemed to welcome it.

Upon settling into their new town, the Potters mostly kept to themselves and their limited social interactions did not win them any friends. The townsfolk found Buddy's waxing lyrical about his tours in Vietnam, his tall tales of being a prisoner of war, and his endless bragging about his many medals tiresome, and likely exaggerated. It was hard to believe this gun-toting buffoon was ever in the CIA. Of course, Buddy clammed up whenever questioned about it, claiming that it was all still highly classified information. He did, however, make sure he was armed at all times, carrying his handguns two at a time in leather holsters, even when he was just pottering around the house or gardening.

Jenelle did not find it any easier to make friends in Mountain City than she had in Pennsylvania. Like many small towns, most of the locals had lived there for generations and they could be slow to warm to outsiders. The family was considered odd, especially Jenelle who didn't have a job or drive a car and seemed to be treated like a small child by her parents. When they went out, Jenelle freaked out the townsfolk by being overly familiar with them, acting as if she knew them, and sometimes even going in for an unwelcome hug.

Like so many socially awkward young people, social media became Jenelle's lifeline. While her disabilities prevented her from establishing a rapport with her peers in real life, she found it was much easier to communicate in online chat rooms and forums. Myspace became her space, and she used pictures of unicorns and butterflies to express the multiple facets of her personality. Softly filtered rainbows and clouds covered most of the background of each picture. The images reinforced Jenelle's identity as something more than just a girl with disabilities; they were an expression of her personality, parts of herself that she couldn't find words for, but hoped other people would be able to understand completely. The kitsch of the design clashed with the earnest text and numerous religious quotations. "I'm a proud Christian Girl" glittered prominently in the middle of her home page.

As Janelle fine-tuned her online persona, she crafted a

backstory for herself. Her introduction read: *I'm a very loving and caring person. I have been told I'm too nice and so sweet. I love to have fun, but I don't drink or party at all. I joke a lot and I'm silly at times. But sometimes I do take things to heart and let things get to me. I try not to, but it's very hard.*

Myspace had a basic profile questionnaire, which Jenelle filled out very thoroughly. She listed her occupation as "being a loving girlfriend" and there were several photos of Jenelle and her parents with a young man whom she tagged as "David." In a couple of these shots, the man had his arm around Jenelle.

He's my boyfriend and my heart and everything, Jenelle wrote. *He has been there for me also. He has been the best thing to happen in my life. I love him to death. We both love each other so much. I don't know what I would do without him.*

She filled out quizzes about her boyfriend and their relationship in which she expressed her hope that they would marry someday. According to one of these quizzes, she had never seen him in his underwear, so it could safely be assumed that the two had not slept together.

She wrote often about her love for her parents, calling them her "heroes" and "the best Momma and Daddy in the world."

Other parts of Jenelle's profile contained gushing comments about her "dear friends" who loved her and looked after her and told her how sweet she was. She referred to them by name and made comments like "they are true best friends" and she hinted that they had weathered dark times together, supporting each other through tragic deaths of members of their friendship circle.

Jenelle's sparkly, gushing Myspace page did not seem to bear much resemblance to reality. She certainly wouldn't be the first person to exaggerate their quality of life on social media, but the friends she referred to were either nonexistent, or the close relationships were imaginary. Jenelle would claim any person she had even the slightest passing interaction with as her closest, most trusted friend.

"I love the friends that I have down here," she wrote of her move to Tennessee. "They are just as sweet and they are wonderful people." But, in truth, Jenelle had no friends in Mountain City. In the world of social media, however, nobody needed to know that.

Soon, a newer, shinier social media platform came along. Facebook was still in its infancy, but the "Add friends" feature appealed to Jenelle. She joined Facebook with gusto, but her mother carefully monitored her page on the computer they shared. In her introduction, Jenelle wrote again of her many friends and their opinions that she was sweet, caring and loving.

Jenelle set about adding everyone she knew, as well as several people she didn't, as Facebook friends.

6

TOPIX

Whereas online negativity seems to dissipate naturally in a large city, it often grates like steel wool in a small town where insults are not easily forgotten.

— A.G. SULZBERGER, "IN SMALL TOWNS, GOSSIP MOVES TO THE WEB, AND TURNS VICIOUS," *THE NEW YORK TIMES,* 2011

When Facebook was still in its infancy, the online public forum Topix was where most of the Millennial generation of Mountain City gathered to exchange news and information, make social plans, and, most of all, gossip.

Topix was a community news forum that provided groups for people from a particular locality to join, much like Facebook's local neighborhood groups we know today. The site crawled the web for local news, then reposted it for people to comment on. Users could start new posts on any topic that they wanted, and others could comment on them. Topix could be used to arrange social gatherings, raise awareness of events in the area, or discuss just about anything, from last night's TV to current politics. The idea was that it would act like a community bulletin board, accessible to anybody.

Unfortunately, the Topix forums were largely unmoderated, and soon became a breeding ground for rumor, slander, bitchiness, and cyberbullying. Users could invent any name they liked and post about other people anonymously. Many people referred to it as the "social media sewer." It was much like 4chan is today.

For such a small town, the Mountain City Topix board was extremely busy, and a virtual hotbed of gossip. Alongside the weather, horoscopes, and news of the next Bible study gathering or updates on City Hall, there were threads started about different residents of the town that had no purpose other than to stir up trouble. It was populated by a lot of teenagers and so it was not unusual to see a thread topic like "Who is the cutest couple in Johnson City High School?" complete with speculation about whether they were having sex. Other such posts included "3 most annoying girls at JCHS" followed by dozens of comments about the stupid way Kendra swung her hair around, and how annoying it was when Kristin batted her eyes when boys were nearby. Other threads had no problem naming someone local and accusing them of being a thief or even a pedophile. The administrators of Topix didn't seem too worried about defamation suits, and rarely made any move to censor or delete the offending posts.

One of the biggest scandals to be rehashed for years was that of the Johnson City school bus driver who was charged with inappropriate touching of a student. The forums were ablaze with speculation about what really happened between the 67-year-old Mountain City bus driver and the teenager who asked him for a cigarette, with many coming to the defense of the man and claiming the girl had instigated the occurrence. Pages and pages of posts let people play judge and jury in a matter they knew little about.

There were also constant polls, like "Who is the best fighter in Mountain City?" or queries about the "best-looking women" in Village Apartments or Shoun's Manor, low-income housing complexes that had dubious reputations for crime and drug activity. Another constant was the litany of people being accused of cheating on their spouses. Then there was the "Johnson County Snitch List," which contained page after page of the names of people others believed to be "narcs" in the local community of drug users and dealers, as well as several "slut lists" full of disparaging discussion about certain women in town.

All in all, it was a mean-spirited cesspool of slander and innuendo. But it was the place to be if you wanted to know what was going on in Mountain City.

7

IRL FRIENDS

Despite her active online life, Jenelle still desperately craved the approval and affection of people in real life (or "IRL" in social media speak). That opportunity came in 2009, when she was filling some of the Potter family's multitude of prescriptions at the pharmacy, and the clerk at the counter struck up a conversation with her. Tracy Greenwell knew Jenelle didn't get out alone much, was often unwell, and seemed to live an extremely sheltered life for a grown woman. After their first meeting, Jenelle sent Tracy a Facebook friend request, and they began speaking on the phone often.

Tracy wanted to bring Jenelle along on outings with her friends, but was surprised when the 27-year-old Jenelle told her that, before she could go anywhere, Tracy would have to visit the Potter residence a couple of times so that Jenelle's parents, Buddy and Barbara, could vet her. Once they got to know her, and if they approved of her, Jenelle would be allowed to go out, providing there would be no drinking or drug-taking involved.

Tracy felt sorry for the awkward Jenelle, whose family

hadn't had much luck integrating with the locals, so she made the effort to visit the Potter residence and charm Jenelle's parents. She must have made a good enough impression, because Jenelle was allowed to accompany her on various outings. She even got Jenelle to try rock climbing, which was quite an achievement, given Jenelle's disabilities and her fear of heights. During that outing, Tracy introduced Jenelle to her brother, Bill Payne. A photo of that day shows a beaming Jenelle being helped into her climbing harness by Bill. The friend group soon suspected that Jenelle had a crush on the affable young man.

Bill did not reciprocate Jenelle's feelings, but he and Tracy thought that their cousin Jamie Curd would make a fine match for Jenelle. Jamie was in his mid-thirties and lived on Pleasant Valley Road with his mother in a ramshackle trailer, at the end of a muddy driveway at the top of a steep hill. With an outdoor laundry tub and a sofa on the porch, it was typical of the dwellings of those who had it the roughest in Johnson County. Jamie had dropped out of school early to go to work at Parkdale Mills, the major employer of young men in the town, and to care for his family, most of whom were unwell. The work was intensely physical, involving climbing up and down the multistory machines, and Jamie worked twelve-hour shifts. By 2009, much of Jamie's meager paycheck went to covering his mother's medication. His father had died some time ago, as had one of his brothers, with Jamie acting as their caretaker until then. His other brother worked with him at the plant, along with his cousin, Bill Payne.

Bill and Jamie were close, with a relationship that was more like brothers than cousins. When they weren't working, they often got together to drink or pop pills. The two got along well, despite their differences. Bill was a wild party guy and had a reputation for being a man about town, while Jamie was slow-witted and didn't have his cousin's charisma or popularity with the ladies. At 35 years old, he had never had a proper girlfriend and stammered when he spoke to most people. He also suffered from a condition that meant he needed to wear dark glasses all the time, even inside.

Jamie was the sort of person other people didn't notice much. If they did, they thought him pleasant, harmless, meek and quiet, not like his gregarious cousin. A follower, not a leader. Bill, on the other hand, was popular, with lots of interests and hobbies. He was a coin collector who enjoyed NASCAR racing, occasional trips to Las Vegas, and had a reputation as a bit of a player with the ladies. He certainly liked to enjoy life and had a tendency to blow his entire paycheck as soon as he got it.

Bill and Tracy secretly thought the two lonely misfits, Jenelle and Jamie, should get together, as there weren't too many other options for them in the town. At 6 foot 2 inches, Jamie was also one of the few guys around who was taller than Jenelle.

Their first meeting was nothing spectacular but, a few days later, Jamie was at Bill's house when Jenelle called to ask for Jamie's number. Bill passed the phone to his cousin, who was only too happy to give his number to a girl.

Jenelle called Jamie often after that, but the calls were extremely brief—no more than forty-five seconds. She explained that she did not want her parents to know that she was calling him, and so had to snatch the odd minute here and there. It was the beginning of an odd and dysfunctional relationship, but it was the first time Jamie had had a proper girlfriend, so it worked for him. He looked forward to Jenelle's odd little phone calls and hoped that, in time, he could meet the rest of the Potter family and take her out for real. Jenelle was a good Christian girl who disapproved of drinking and drugs, so Jamie hid that part of his life from her.

When Jenelle mentioned she was having computer problems, he saw an opportunity to get inside the Potter residence. Jamie was known around town as someone who enjoyed tinkering with computers and often fixed basic problems for people. He told Jenelle he thought he'd be able to fix hers, and she arranged for him to come over and check it out.

Once he arrived, Jamie discovered there was just one computer in the house, in a common area where both Barbara and Jenelle could use it. Buddy seemed to have no interest in it. Barbara provided Jamie with a list of things that needed fixing and complained of it running slowly. Jamie used the family's lack of technical knowledge as an excuse to visit the Potter household several times, cleaning up their hard drive and eventually reformatting it. While he worked on the computer in the poky office, surrounded by various boxes, papers, and junk that hinted at hoarding issues, Jenelle sat and talked with him. However, while Barbara and Buddy accepted his help with the computer and tolerated him being around, they did not approve of him and certainly didn't think he was good enough to be a boyfriend to their beloved daughter. There was no way they would allow her to date him, so the relationship had to remain a secret, mostly carried out on the telephone in those bizarre short bursts.

As Jamie's feelings for Jenelle developed, he hit on an idea that would allow them to speak more often. Jamie bought Jenelle a prepaid cell phone, and, rather than risk smuggling it in, he hid for her in a bush at the corner of her front yard. Jenelle retrieved it when she was sure here parents weren't watching. From then on, whenever she got a moment alone, she and Jamie talked on the phone, sometimes for hours at a time. This arrangement worked until Barbara found the illicit cell phone and sent Jamie a text message letting him know she was "on to him." Jamie was frustrated, but he remained determined to win over Jenelle's parents so that the two of them could be together. He knew this would be no simple task, as Jenelle had already told him that Buddy had once been in the CIA, though it was Barbara who frightened Jamie the most.

Undeterred, Jamie bought a second cell phone, which he again left in the bush for Jenelle to retrieve. After secretly speaking for five or six months, Jamie and Jenelle began to talk about eloping.

When she wasn't on the phone to Jamie, Jenelle was on the computer. She was much more confident when she was posting on social media or in the Topix forums, as people did not judge her by her disabilities. She read through all the threads on Topix, some of which became quite heated. Something about the high-school mentality of them attracted her. She soon compiled a list of girls she considered "mean girls." Sometimes she posted what she thought of them on her Facebook page, and other times she posted on Topix, where she didn't have to use her real name.

8

BILL AND BILLIE JEAN

I n late 2009, a new girl started working at the textile plant alongside Bill and Jamie. Her name was Billie Jean Hayworth, and she was a slight, pretty brunette with a friendly, outgoing nature. Her love of running and volleyball kept her fit and slender. She loved nothing more than to dress up and goof around, and she had a close group of friends and family she liked to spend time with. She clicked with Bill immediately and he was quickly smitten. They had many shared interests, both being lovers of the outdoors who enjoyed fishing, hiking, camping, and running, as well as perusing flea markets, yard sales, and auctions. Bill told his cousin that he and Billie Jean hit it off right away, and that there was no stopping him falling head over heels in love with her. They never ran out of things to talk and laugh about.

Jamie noticed a change in Bill after he began dating Billie Jean. Bill had had his share of run-ins with the law, but once he met Billie, he made an effort to clean himself up. He began drinking less and made an effort to reduce the partying. He stopped trying to be a ladies' man and had eyes only for Billie Jean.

When Jamie spoke to Jenelle about the new relationship, she dismissed it, saying that Billie Jean was just the latest of Bill's many women and he would soon tire of her. However, on the contrary, their relationship intensified, and the couple soon spent every possible moment together.

Meanwhile, Jamie and Jenelle's most unusual relationship continued, with the two of them still having to sneak around and hide from Jenelle's disapproving parents. They had noticed that Jamie was keen on Jenelle, but Barbara in particular thought that he didn't measure up as a suitor for her daughter and did what she could to come between them. Matters came to a head in February 2010, when police called the Potter residence to say they had found Jenelle wandering in the dark and Buddy had to fetch her and drive her home.

Apparently Jenelle thought she and Jamie were going to elope that night, which was also his birthday, and had sneaked out of the house to meet him. Jamie, however, had been drinking at his cousin Bill's house and he had passed out on the couch, seemingly oblivious to the marriage plan. At 8:30 the next morning, he answered his phone to an enraged Buddy thundering down the line that Jenelle didn't love him and that he should stay away from her if he knew what was good for him. He then passed the phone to Jenelle, who confirmed what Buddy had said.

Although Jamie agreed to stop talking to Jenelle, she called him three days later and assured him she loved him and wanted to keep their secret relationship going. They went back to their old ways, speaking on the phone for hours, sometimes all night long, and when they weren't speaking, they were texting. Because Jenelle didn't want her mother to know they were talking, she contacted Jamie at odd hours and told him never to call her. Although Jamie considered Jenelle his girlfriend, they were yet to go on a single date.

Bill eventually introduced Billie Jean to Jenelle, who quickly added her on Facebook. She also added Billie Jean's best friend, Lindsey Thomas, even though she had never met her, as well as another friend of Billie Jean's, Tara Osborne, after meeting her at the grocery store. The three women soon found themselves on the receiving end of incessant private messages from Jenelle every time they logged onto Facebook. They tried to mitigate this by changing their status so that it wouldn't show when they were online, but Jenelle filled their inboxes with messages anyway. Many of her messages were asking why they hadn't responded to previous messages, pointing out that they clearly had plenty of time to do so, as they'd recently posted on their pages or liked and commented on other posts.

Jenelle had a habit of being overbearing with new friends, which people understandably found off-putting. She not only sent private messages over Facebook, but called people on the phone or bombarded them with text messages. If she felt slighted, she responded disproportionately to whatever insult she felt had been directed at her. She was particularly offended by Lindsey and Billie Jean, who, after growing increasingly annoyed by her constant messages and calls, had begun avoiding her. Eventually, Bill, Billie Jean, and Lindsey all unfriended her on Facebook. In retaliation, Jenelle began posting in groups or on her own wall, saying that the two women were "mean."

When Tara tried to let Jenelle down more gently, saying she hadn't responded to Jenelle's messages because she had problems with her computer, Jenelle responded with a long

message that began: "Hey, sweetie, it's really okay. I understand," but then descended into a rant about the "mean
girls," writing: *If they don't stop talking and putting me down,
I'm going to end up saying what I'm really thinking and how
mad I really am and see how they like it. I have not done
anything to anyone and I stay to myself and talk to friends. But
they go overboard and they are just mean girls, really. I hate they
talk about me and I hate they act like they do—anything to
anyone to get away with it. It's sad.*

Jenelle continued to barrage Tara, until she, too,
removed Jenelle as a friend from her Facebook account.
However, Jenelle could still send private messages, and she
immediately did so, demanding to know why. Still trying to
be diplomatic, Tara responded that she had decided to
reserve her Facebook account for only family and close
friends. She wrote, "Don't take it to heart, I don't mean
anything by it."

Jenelle responded that she understood and thanked Tara
for getting back to her, but, shortly after, Tara received
another message accusing her of harassment, making
anonymous phone calls and messing with Jenelle's mailbox.
Tara called Jenelle and told her that her accusations were
ridiculous, and then told Jenelle the truth about exactly why
she had unfriended her, saying she was tired of her drama
and the unkind and untrue things she was posting about
Tara's friends.

Jenelle's interminable posting about the mean girls
intensified not long after Bill and Billie Jean took their relationship to the next level and moved in together with Bill's
father, Paw Bill. Things had moved rather fast, but there was
good reason for it ... Billie Jean had discovered that she was
pregnant with Bill's baby.

Bill was overjoyed. He already had a son from a previous

relationship, but the boy had moved to Florida with his mother and Bill did not have much of a role in his life. He was determined that this time it was going to be different. The opioid and meth crisis had hit the local area and Bill hard, but he enrolled in a Suboxone clinic to help him curtail his drug habit. To the surprise of all who knew him, he even gave up smoking for the sake of the health of the forthcoming baby.

Billie Jean was excited and nervous about this sudden change in her life, but she looked forward to the new adventure she had to share with Bill.

9

THE TOPIX FEUD

I normally don't post anything on these forums, but as I look at them it makes me wonder why there's so much hostility. Shouldn't these sites be used for community events and announcements? Looks as though people have more time to mind everyone else's business besides their own!!!

— TOPIX POST, MOUNTAIN CITY
COMMUNITY

Not long after Bill and Billie Jean went public with their joyous news, vile anonymous comments about the couple, as well as Billie's friends, started to appear in Facebook groups and on the Mountain City page of Topix. It started with someone calling himself "Matt Potter." Matt's Topix posts were all concentrated on denigrating Billie Jean and her two friends, Lindsey Thomas and Tara Osborne. He called them "no good whores" and accused the women of selling drugs. He made numerous threats of violence against the trio.

Soon someone posting as "Kelly" weighed in,

responding to support Matt's accusations and threats, adding that Lindsey had HIV. Matt and Kelly's only posts on the forum were to attack Billie Jean and her friends, and to defend Jenelle Potter.

The rants were disturbingly vicious, and riddled with spelling, punctuation, and grammatical errors. One read [errors fixed for readability]: *Just die. She is a waste being on earth ... Damn whore. They're all whores and always will be and you can't make them into wives when they have 10 more men they sleep with. They are not happy and they want everyone else not to be happy. Fuck them. I'm happy Jenelle is so sweet caring and will stand up for herself. What's Lindsey and Billie Jean do? Nothing but lie and try to get others hurt. Fuck them I hope they die die—and that baby, and Bill.*

Bill's sister, Tracy Greenwell, who had been the first to bring Jenelle into their friendship group, sent a message to Jenelle on Facebook, saying: *Your friend Matt needs to leave Billie Jean and Lindsey off of the Topix website. You lost my brother as a friend and I'm not happy with you either.*

Jenelle responded by denying that she had anything to do with the posts by "Matt Potter" and that she couldn't help it if people wanted to chime in and defend her when she had done nothing wrong, claiming there had been "a lot of trash talking about me in town from both of them." She also alleged that she was being harassed, not just online, but in real life too. Jenelle told Tracy: *They need to back off. I don't talk to them and don't know them. Why don't you tell them to get away from me and tell them do not pull in my driveway. Dad is getting a little sick of it. He has gone with me to the cops and I showed them and gave names and they looked everything up and they also know that I'm not doing a thing. So, this is not my fault. If you hate me then I don't care.*

Lindsey also telephoned Jenelle and asked for a truce, in

an effort to end the relentless disparaging accusations being directed at her. Jenelle denied being the author of the Topix posts and, bizarrely, denied being the author of the posts on her own Facebook page, claiming she had been hacked.

Lindsey then started receiving calls that caller ID revealed came from the Potter house. The calls were usually just someone breathing down the line without speaking. Both Billie Jean and Tara also received countless annoying phone calls, all the while continuing to be on the receiving end of vicious comments all over social media. Tara Osborne even filed for an order of protection against Jenelle, citing "many annoying phone calls from the Potter residence." However, as the process was unfamiliar to her, she filed the paperwork incorrectly and found she got little cooperation from the Sheriff's Department.

Sometimes the friends were together at Billie Jean's house when Jenelle called repeatedly. Eventually, Billie Jean had to take the phone off the hook to prevent further calls. Billie Jean became increasingly bothered by the harassment, but, as she was heavily pregnant, she felt it was not the best time to cause drama or fight back.

When Tara's nuisance case was dismissed because she did not have a close enough relationship with Jenelle to warrant the order, Lindsey Thomas filed her own phone harassment charge against Jenelle in the Johnson County General Sessions Court, also claiming to have received many calls from the increasingly unstable woman. Both Billie Jean and Tara agreed to be a witness in Lindsey's case.

Lindsey's affidavit alleged: *Jenelle Potter, whom I've never met, has been harassing me for months now. She has called my phone anywhere from 5 to 20 times a day. I have asked her on more than one occasion to quit calling me, but have had no luck. This all started because I deleted her off my Facebook. She*

*continues to lie and say stuff about me all over her Facebook. I
have proof of phone calls and stuff on Facebook.*

The harassment cases became the talk of the town, at
least on social media and the Topix forums. Someone
calling themselves "sneakypete" began a thread called
"Jenelle Potter strikes again" on April 2, 2011. The topic was
clearly intended to stir up trouble, with the opening
message reading: "Heard someone's taking her to court and
now she's playing innocent..."

"Is she picking fights with other girls in town again?"
asked a poster by the name of "dylan80."

"Apparently she's accusing someone of throwing trash in
her yard and some other stuff. I think she's just out for attention. And she's batshit crazy," replied sneakypete.

Jenelle told anyone who listened that it was her who was
being relentlessly tormented and harassed by the three
women, and that the filing of the charges against her was all
part of the victimization of her by the "mean girls." She also
claimed to have several male friends who thought of Jenelle
as their little sister, who stood up for and defended her.

She showed Jamie an email from one such friend, Brian
G. She told Jamie that Brian had forwarded her a message
from one of her tormentors, which contained vile language
and vicious attacks on Jenelle's looks and weight, referenced
her apparent friendship with a pedophile, and claimed that
Jamie secretly despised her. "Eww she is so ugly anyways
just look at her ugly face. And her Body eww she is sooo fat
and she needs to lose a lot of weight," the nasty note had
said. "She is just a little ass hole, and she might be smart but
she is ugly in every way. YUCK YUCK. she looks like a damn
duck. I hope she gets killed soon. Billie Jean and Lindsey, let
this get back to her."

When forwarding the message to Jenelle, "Brian G" had

assured her that he and several other old friends were mad on her behalf. "We all grew up together as great friends. God Jenelle, you're wonderful, sweet, caring, kind hearted and will do anything for anyone."

These supporters of Jenelle coincidentally used many of the same phrases and made the same spelling and grammar errors that Jenelle made.

Meanwhile, the postings on Topix were becoming increasingly vitriolic, as new people entered the argument and took sides. Someone called "Dan White" joined in to support Matt and Kelly against Jenelle's enemies.

Dan wrote: *I know Billie, that Bitch has lived with more guys and had sex with 80 per cent of Mountain City. And Lindsey I would say half of Mountain City... she has been all over and she does have HIV, this is all around town. And Tara, she will give it to anyone ... She is a whore, too. I agree with you both. And this girl, Jenelle, I do know in passing, but she is a good girl and was brought up right, you can tell ... she just a sweet girl. I will be praying for Jenelle. As far as the others go, they're no good whore sluts who are carrying something and giving it to everyone. Damn girls. They live in high school still and they need to grow up.*

Matt responded: *Jenelle is a sweet person and people try to get her. But she has a lot of us behind her, if she knows us or not. But her dad is Big Time and he will deal with the rest of this shit. They're fucking whores and that's all this town is, and drugs. I know for sure Billie Jean and Lindsey did drugs together and I know Lindsey does meth she gets off Jason. I know way too much lol. I love that Jenelle is not like them, she stayed sweet ... they are dumb assholes, mother fuckers getting what's coming their way, and they don't know who I am.*

That same day, Jenelle sent her mother, Barbara, an email with the subject line, "what Lindsey said." The email appeared to contain the text of a vicious message sent from Lindsey to Jenelle. The message called Jenelle names and threatened her: *your ass is mine. You're a fucking bitch, remember that I can get you and will. Your daddy can't do shit to me. I'm above the law, dumb fucking bitch.*

Buddy and Barbara had no doubt that their Jenelle was the innocent victim in the escalating feud. They spoke to Bill Payne on the phone, who told them it was Jenelle who was causing all the trouble, and he asked them to stop her from writing vicious lies about him and his heavily pregnant partner. Jenelle denied to her parents that she was behind the nasty comments.

The next day, Matt was back on Topix, writing: *Well I guess Billy Clay knows they have his number and his phone is being tapped. Ha. I know what he said about Jenelle and it was wrong. He's a fucking work ... I'm going to be posting numbers if they don't stop bugging Jenelle. And then all kinds of people will be calling them. I have cells and home phone numbers, and fucking Billie Jean is getting so fat with that baby she looks like a chipmunk that's been eating too many nuts. LOL. I hope she loses that baby. It don't need a mother like Billie Jean. And Billy Clay, he's no father by the way he acts and talks. Sooner they move out of town the better ... I hope they have to live out in the woods. More better for chipmunk, she can make friends out there and fuck deer and bear and whatever else. I hope a bear eats her, but the way she looks it would go running the other way LOL. Ugly ass bitch whore. Can't leave no one alone. Druggie whore ass bitch. Go fuck a damn tree for all I care. Leave Jenelle alone.*

The feud continued to escalate, and the Potters became regular visitors to the local police station, as they lodged complaints about the various people they claimed were victimizing Jenelle. On one occasion, the police attended the Potter residence to investigate a rock that had allegedly been thrown at the house. The rock in question had "Billy Payne" written on one side and "Billie Jean" on the other, as well as the quote "I'm your huckleberry." The police thought it very odd that the rock throwers would sign their names on the rocks that were thrown at the Potter house like that, and so struggled to take the allegations seriously.

Sheriff Mike Reece also didn't know how to respond when Buddy Potter came to his office to make a formal complaint about a county official unfriending his daughter on Facebook, or what to make of Buddy's claim that he used to work for the CIA. The sheriff just told him that unfriending someone was not illegal and ushered him out of the office.

10

ENTER CHRIS

J enelle's dramas may have been escalating, but things were getting better on the romantic front and at home. In May 2011, Jamie's mother passed away, leaving Jamie, who had nursed her since she became sick, inconsolable. It touched him when Buddy called him to offer his condolences and then told him that, if he ever needed anything, the Potters were there for him. Barbara also called him and invited him to dinner.

Jamie must have made a good impression, because Barbara began inviting him to the house on holidays. That helped pull Jamie out of the depression he had fallen into after his mother's death, and it eased his crushing loneliness, now that he was living in the rundown house alone. It meant spending more time with Jenelle and the couple could sometimes steal kisses in the computer room.

Buddy's tales of being in the military and working for the CIA impressed Jamie. Buddy talked about his missions in other countries, and Jamie knew Buddy owned many guns, at least two of which he carried at all times—one in a shoulder holster and one on his ankle. Sometimes he wore a

double holster on his hips, Old West gunslinger-style.
Barbara also sang Buddy's praises, warning that he could
kill a man a dozen different ways if he were so inclined.

Barbara and Jenelle brought Jamie up to speed on the
trouble they were having with the local girls, whom they
believed were targeting Jenelle because they were jealous of
how pretty she was. Every time Jamie visited, Barbara
monopolized the conversation, ranting about the other girls
in town whom she saw as Jenelle's tormentors. Jamie didn't
have Facebook, so Jenelle forwarded Jamie some messages
they'd sent to her.

One said: *You're a fucking bitch and you know your fucking
ass is going to jail and Bill is going to kill you he has said that and
I hope he does. None of us want you around nor living. Your a
waste of air and time on everyone. You are nothing. You really
think you are sweet and smart HAHA yeah right your dumb and
very ugly, no one wants you. Billie thinks your fat, and Bill. Me,
fucking Lindsey, I just hate you're alive. You will die bitch and I
cant wait to see it. Go to hell bitch.*

Another said: *Jenelle I will get you no good bitch ... I'm
fucking Lindsey remember that. I know everything you talk
about in your email to someone named Chris. Who is that you
fucking bitch? Your daddy cant do shit to me. I'm above the law,
dumb fucking bitch.*

The venomous abuse being hurled at Jenelle shocked
Jamie, especially as Jenelle never used foul language like
that. She was such a good girl that Jamie had tried as best he
could to clean up his own language and habits to be worthy
of her and, hopefully, eventually gain the approval of her
parents. He didn't seem to find it strange that Lindsey
repeatedly identified herself as "fucking Lindsey."

Jamie was still working at the plant with Bill, but
tensions were rising between two cousins. Bill was furious

that he had shared concerns with Jamie and later found parts of their conversation posted on Topix, which meant Jamie had probably run and told Jenelle. The bad blood between the two was enough that their employer began assigning them to different shifts.

In her conversations with Jamie, Jenelle occasionally mentioned her sister, Christie, saying that she had been cruel and abusive to her throughout her childhood, locking her in a dog kennel and calling her names.

Although they rarely brought up their other daughter, Barbara and Buddy talked about someone called Chris, who Barbara referred to as her son. Jenelle explained to Jamie that she had known Chris most of her life and that he treated her like a little sister. She said Chris used to drive her to high school and pick her up after track practice. He was very protective of her, and, like Buddy, was a CIA agent from Pennsylvania who had transferred to Tennessee. Unlike Buddy, though, Chris still had an active role in the CIA. He wrote to her every day and she had filled him in on the dramas she had been having in Mountain City.

Barbara also corresponded with Chris about the threats and abuse directed at her daughter. She was sick and tired of their antics and was ready for Buddy and Chris to use their CIA training to do something about it. She just needed the CIA to provide Buddy with his new ID, and he was good to go. Barbara told Chris in one email that Buddy "... is fed up & ready. Shame they had to push him to this because he is a very patient man, but once you push him too hard too long, it's over." She told Jamie that Chris was monitoring the family and would do *anything* to protect Jenelle.

Now that she had accepted Jamie as a family friend, Barbara began to write long, rambling emails to him about how her family was being targeted. Sometimes she shared some of the messages she and Chris exchanged. They often referred to the ongoing court saga between Lindsey and Jenelle, and to Jenelle's fear of going to jail over it all, which she believed would inevitably kill her. The Potter family lived in fear of multiple people, convinced that there were many folk in town who would harm Jenelle should the opportunity arise. The emails sometimes ran to more than ten pages and were often so repetitive that Jamie just skimmed the pages to see if she had anything new or important to say.

Soon Chris began emailing and text messaging Jamie directly, confirming what Jenelle was saying about the ongoing campaign of harassment against her on Topix and Facebook. Chris told him it really needed to stop. All of Chris's emails came via Jenelle's account, BUL2DOG@aol.com, so as to not compromise his CIA credentials.

Chris started emails with "Hey, man," or "Hey, dude, how's it going?" and he would, as Jamie later said, "rant and rave about everything" in his emails. He cursed, called people names, and wished harm on others. Chris's hatred was mostly directed at Bill, Billie Jean, Lindsey, and their friends, and he used foul language and insults when talking about them. All of Chris's messages were centered on Jenelle, how sweet and wonderful she was, how persecuted she had been, and how her protection was a top priority of the CIA.

Chris also mentioned that Jenelle had confided in him about how much she cared for Jamie. Soon Chris was giving Jamie advice on how he could improve the relationship, which involved buying Jenelle gifts and declaring his love repeatedly.

Jamie was being invited to the Potter residence more frequently, and each time Barbara and Buddy brought him up to speed on who was emailing what, and all the nasty things that they'd said about Jenelle. Barbara characterized it as being "like a war." Buddy shook his head and stated that he did not understand why they were doing it and that he just wanted it to stop. Jenelle often came home in tears, with harrowing tales of plots to harm her, to kidnap and rape her, and to hurt her family. Barbara started demanding to know from Jamie and Buddy what they were going to do about it.

While Jenelle was present during these conversations, she remained silent. Jamie noted that, when she spoke to him on the phone, Jenelle was opinionated about things, but when she was around her parents, she acted needy and childlike. Jamie had fallen in love with Jenelle, but was still nervous around her parents. Jenelle's mother especially intimidated him, and he walked on eggshells around her, hoping not to anger her or set her off. He listened to her tirades patiently, nodding and agreeing, in the hopes that it would earn him an invitation to dinner or a family outing.

Jenelle was desperately worried about the looming court case and terrified of a criminal conviction that might send her to prison. The emails from Chris to Jamie at that time were full of concern about Janelle, who would occasionally be hospitalized due to the stress. "I hope she don't think about killing herself," he wrote.

Jamie responded: *I think that if it wasn't for us she might have thought about it, didn't say it, but I can tell she has just took all she can take from those motherfuckers. They won't let up and they're crazy. Hell, I don't know why they have to do this. I don't know how their life has got to such at the point that they see this as a sick joke ... dumb bastards.*

Around that time Jamie presented Jenelle with a ring. He later said it wasn't an engagement ring, just a ring that she had wanted. He would get her anything she wanted if it was within his power.

During one visit, Barbara warned Jamie that Jenelle's enemies were planning on targeting him too. However, emails from Chris assured him, "I've got your back." Chris claimed he had Lindsey under twenty-four hour surveillance and that he had "shot her back glass out of her car." Jenelle confirmed Chris had told her he was watching over Jamie too, and had even followed him around town one day to make sure none of their tormentors got to him.

Chris wrote in one email to Barbara, "I'm sure it's getting to Jenelle. She is going to die here I feel with all this crap." He then said that if Buddy decided to do anything about it, he should "get Bill first" because "he's really mean and an asshole. Damn fucker." Barbara dutifully printed out the emails so that Buddy could read them.

11

A NEW ARRIVAL

Despite the many, many ill wishes expressed toward Billie Jean's pregnancy on Topix, in mid-2011, baby Tyler came into the world and his parents were immediately besotted. According to Billie Jean's best friend, in an interview with TV show *20/20*, "He was her world. The glow she had about her when he came into the world was just unbelievable."

Paw Bill could not have been a happier man. He had his son and future daughter-in-law safely at home, and now this little bundle of joy had come into his world. Paw Bill's heart was full.

But not everybody was happy. The vitriol on Topix ramped up considerably after the birth of baby Tyler.

"Mike Dunn" posted: *I'm about to fight with you Billie, why don't you shut up your fucking mouth you Bitch. One day girl you are going to get beat up really good and left for dead. You better shut up you bitch. Go fuck a cow for all I care. Damn hooker, slut bag whore .... And your bastard baby take it with you and leave this fucking town. You won't leave here alive.*

Matt Potter posted a response: *Damn I think we just need*

*to gut her and leave her for dead and kill the damn fucking whore
... you're a fucking no good person and your day is coming.*

The local townspeople had become aware of the
ongoing feud, not just via Topix, which was mostly read by
younger people, but because the Potters would often tell
strangers about it in an attempt to gain their sympathy.
However, the incidents the townsfolk witnessed often didn't
exactly align with the Potters' version of events.

One afternoon, Linda Stephens was putting a Hot Pocket
into the microwave at the convenience store where she
worked, when she heard a commotion outside. Billie Jean
was pumping gas when her car was blocked by another
vehicle pulling in between the gas pumps and the store. The
occupants began screaming at the new mother. Linda saw
Barbara and Jenelle Potter gesticulating and pointing as they
shrieked at Billie that she was "white trash" who "don't
deserve to be a mother!" Linda went to the door and asked a
visibly distressed Billie Jean if she was OK, and whether she
wanted her to call the police. At the mention of police, the
car carrying Barbara and Jenelle took off up the road toward
Mountain City.

Billie Jean was shaken and upset, but was mostly
concerned for her baby, who was still in the car on the way
to his first pediatric visit. "This won't stop," she wailed to
Linda. "They follow me everywhere. Now that I'm a mother,
they say I'm unfit. They call me trash. They're constantly
threatening me." She was so shaken that she paid with a
twenty-dollar bill and forgot to grab the change before she
rushed home to get her fiancé to accompany her to the
appointment. She was terrified that the Potters might
confront her there as well, if she were to go alone.

Jenelle posted on her social media that Lindsey, Bill,
Billie Jean and "a few others" had threatened to kill her and

then Buddy. She wrote: *But it came out they dont like me b/c i'm smart and i'm very pretty and the cops are mad b/c they go up there and lie and they they come to me and ask me things. And now they have stoped b/c dad went up there and kicked there butts.*

Jerry "JD" Winebarger, who worked at Food Lion, was often on the receiving end of Buddy Potter's diatribes about the people he claimed were harassing his daughter. Buddy ranted and raved to the shop assistant as though the two men were friends, though JD only knew the Potters as customers of the store. At one point, Buddy said that if he got a chance, he was going to put a bullet through Bill Payne's head. JD didn't think he was serious.

Jenelle tried to rustle up support for her cause by sending messages to acquaintances she hoped would be on her side. One of these was Lyndsey Potter (no relation – Potter was a common surname in the area), a friend of Billie Jean and Lindsey Thomas. Jenelle sent her a private message that said: *I'm not trying to be mean, but your so called friends are still coming after me and I'm never alone, and they have done a lot to my house and to my family, and I'm not mean but I'm getting there. I put that pic of them on once for a few friends to see who they were and I took it down. Do I think they are mean? Yes. Do I think you are fooled? Yes. You need to be careful who you're friends with. Maybe it's not because I'm from here, but I'm sick of this crap and it needs to stop. They need to grow up and live their life like I'm living mine. I'm sick and in the hospital more than I'm at home and they need to stop. I hope you don't think I'm being mean, but it's about time I take up for myself and say what I think for once. I've never done that, wow. I'm 30 and I act more grown up than most people. I have been through too much to let them get to me.*

Lyndsey responded to the message, stating: *Sorry that*

you're sick, but have you actually seen them doing this, or are you just assuming 'cause you want it to be them? I honestly don't believe that they're bothering you. They have much better things to do than to worry about you. Billie Jean just had a baby, so, why in the hell would she be so out to get you? I think the best thing for you to do is to drop it, keep your mouth shut and move on. If they are bothering you then they'll see it isn't working and they'll quit.

Jenelle replied: *No, I know what they are doing and I know other people that have seen it, too. But, I was not going to write you back, but what made me so mad is you think I want to be like them. Yes, a whore and living with guys and sleeping around and drinking and smoking, yeah, right. I love who I am and I have a good life. I'm 30 years old. They can't grow up and they don't even have jobs and they lie . . . and I am so not like that. I don't care that she had her baby. I feel bad for it, a mother like her. I hope maybe it can go to a better home, but the thing is like I say, I know . . . who I am and I love who I am and I'm not from here and I'm smart. People down here never seem to do anything with their lives other than pick and, excuse me, hurt people. I'm not like that. I'm a nice girl and I'm doing the best I can. My health is no one's business, I guess. But, yes, it's . . . bad but I'm grateful for every day that God gives me, so, maybe you should think before you talk.*

Lyndsey responded: *You don't seem very smart to me, but that's my opinion and to each their own. No one is perfect and I'm positive you're definitely not. My advice to you really is to drop it. And you say you're 30 years old, this doesn't seem like a smart 30 year old behavior to me, smart one.*

In a final message, Jenelle replied: *Well, I think they really need to stop their damn games. As far as me being smart it's kind of funny, I got 4.0 out of high school and I'm still smarter than you girls. I don't like you anymore. I thought you were nice, but you are not. And, wow, you're dumb for everything is right in front of you. Let me guess, you do drugs with them. Well, I will block you and I will never talk to you ever again. I think you are no good. Rich whores is what you three are and you need to get over yourselves.*

As was her way, rather than winning a friend, Jenelle had made another enemy.

Jenelle's sister, Christie, had moved to Mountain City to look after her grandmother in 2009, but she had such a fractured relationship with her family that she had taken out an order of protection against them. Specifically, the order was against Barbara, who she thought was a danger not just to Christie but also her grandmother. Barbara was furious, as were Jenelle's mysterious supporters on Topix, who soon started adding Christie's name to their increasingly hateful posts.

12

THE PHONE HARASSMENT COURT CASE

J amie Curd spent his 2011 Thanksgiving and Christmas with the Potters. They were beginning to treat him like family, though Jenelle's parents were still oblivious to their relationship. Nearly all their conversations continued to revolve around Jenelle and the trouble she was having with the locals. The hearing date loomed for Lindsey Thomas's nuisance charge against Jenelle, which had been postponed several times because Jenelle had claimed to be too sick to attend court.

The phone harassment charge was finally heard in general sessions court on November 30, 2011. Billie Jean and Tara were there to support Lindsey and to testify against Jenelle. However, the case was dismissed as Lindsey was not able to satisfy the burden of proof and establish beyond reasonable doubt that the phone calls and online messages originated from Jenelle. The Potter family took this as a decisive victory and proof that Jenelle's version of events was truthful.

After court, Buddy, Barbara, Jenelle, and Jamie—who

had attended court with the Potters—went to a convenience store near Paw Bill's house to have lunch. While they were eating, Billie Jean and Tara came into the store, but did an about-turn when they saw the Potters. When the Potters and Jamie left, Bill Payne pulled into the parking lot, jumped out of his car and began hollering at them, waving a thick folder of papers that he said contained proof that Jenelle was writing hateful comments all over social media about him, Billie Jean, Tara, and Lindsey. He insisted he didn't want trouble, he just wanted it to stop. Jamie left the scene as Bill and Buddy yelled over each other, neither one willing to back down. As far as Buddy was concerned, the court case was resolved in Jenelle's favor, and to him that meant she was innocent of anything and everything she had been accused of. Bill begged him just to read what was in the folder to see what was really going on.

To some of the outsiders looking on, it appeared that Bill and Buddy had simmered down by the end of the confrontation. Before parting ways, Buddy told Bill to call him if anything else occurred and Bill seemed satisfied with the resolution. Bill hoped that would be the end to what had seemed like a never-ending social media saga.

After the public confrontation between Bill and the Potters, Bill called Jamie and told his cousin about the folder which he described as being "about two inches thick" and comprised of emails and posts he had printed from the internet, many of which called him a "bad father who didn't deserve his children." He tried to impress upon Jamie how much it hurt, but he also warned Jamie that he believed that Jenelle was behind many of the usernames that posted on Topix. Bill also told his cousin that he doubted that the elusive "Chris" who messaged Jamie was a real person either. In an effort to get Jamie to believe him, Bill had invented a story, which he told only to Jamie, who later told Jenelle. The very next day, that story appeared in one of the Topix posts under one of the names Bill believed to be an alter ego of Jenelle. Jamie refused to believe that Jenelle was capable of such deception, and the two cousins had another row.

The online feud escalated. Barbara Potter weighed in and took to posting, using Jenelle's account, but identifying herself as "Jenelle's Mom." In one she wrote: *Bill, Lindsey, Billie Jean, Tara, all of you are no good evil friends! Leave Jenelle alone. She won legally in court—the Judge knows you people. Jenelle is not well at all as you all know & she is sick today. I'm asking you nicely to Please Stop the harassment. May God have mercy on Your souls. Thank you... Jenelle's mom ...*

Barbara also wrote to Chris and asked him to make sure that he identified himself as Jenelle's brother whenever he made any posts via Jenelle's page. On 14 December, the mysterious Chris posted a warning via Jenelle's account, writing in all caps: *TO BILL PAYNE, BILLIE JEAN HAYWORTH, LINDSEY THOMAS AND TARA AND BRAD AND ETC: PLEASE LEVE JENELLE ALONE AND STOP WITH THE HARASSMENT AND STOP TRYING TO RUIN HER LIFE. LOOK AT YOUR OWN LIVES AND WORK ON THAT. BECAUSE YOU ALL ARE JUST A BUNCH OF WHITE TRASH NO GOOD UGLY PEOPLE THAT LOVE TO HURT OTHERS ... BILL AND BILLIE JEAN AND LINDSEY GET OFF YOUR METH DRUGS AND STOP GOING AFTER MY SISTER AND MY FAMILY THANK YOU. OR YOU CAN JUST GO JUMP OFF A MOUNTAIN FOR ALL I CARE. YOU ALL NEED TO GET OUT OF MY SISTER'S LIFE.*

Rather than stop, it escalated as Jenelle continued to

post several times a day on Facebook that Lindsey and Billie Jean were "mean" and "whores" and should be "punished." She brought up Billie Jean's baby often and wished harm upon them all. She accused Lindsey of calling her "all the time." Chris and Matt also made numerous appearances on social media, via Jenelle's accounts, and voiced their opinions of the people Jenelle considered her enemies. There were several death threats toward all of them—even Billie Jean's baby. In another message, Barbara claimed that Jenelle's Facebook account had been hacked purely to say mean things about others in town. The hacking was further evidence, in her mind, of the ongoing harassment of her daughter.

Around this time, Jenelle let it slip to Jamie that "she was going to have to start calling Lindsey again." Previously, Jenelle had claimed total innocence, saying that she was the one being harassed with phone calls and that someone had been spoofing her number to call Lindsey. When Jamie pressed Jenelle about this comment, she "got real defensive" and "wouldn't say anything else about it." Jamie let it go, as he was deeply in love with Jenelle and was firmly on the Potters' side in the feud against his cousin, Bill, and his friends. He received a constant barrage of messages from Barbara, Jenelle, and Chris (via Jenelle's account) about the ongoing harassment from the vicious little group that they claimed was driving Jenelle to the brink of suicide. Chris, Barbara, and Buddy discussed what they wanted to do to the people who were making Jenelle's life a living hell, and it was becoming increasingly violent.

Barbara wrote to Jamie, "They are trying to kill Jenelle little by little (but doc says that at this rate, it could happen anytime with a heart attack/stroke ... the stress has to stop)." She said the group would not stop "until we're all dead/gone" and that Chris had told her "the cops are behind Billie Jean and Lindsey." However, Jamie was assured that the CIA had his back, no matter what he decided to do. Barbara had warmed enough to him that she told him to call her "Barbie".

More than anyone, Bill was sick of the drama. He tried to smooth things over with the Potters, tried to reason with them, tried asking Jenelle's parents to please stop her from writing vicious opinions about him, Billie Jean, their baby, and their parenting skills all over social media. His entreaties fell on deaf ears. That wasn't Jenelle, the Potters insisted. She had been hacked. It was Lindsey Thomas. Not their Jenelle. Oh no, Jenelle was sick, she was innocent, she was the victim in all of this.

Frustrated, Bill told the Potters that Jenelle was lying to them, as well as the rest of the world. But they were having none of it.

"Leave us alone," Barbara yelled at Bill. "If you call here again, I'm gonna do something about it."

Soon afterwards, Chris wrote a particularly unhinged email to Barbara, containing some very un-CIA-like language:

Well we know that Bill is Fucking drug head. Yes he has told everyone Buddy is selling drugs LOL like anyone would think that. They need to stop hacking and Lindsey has been down there. Bill lies and everyone knows it, and is always trying to hurt someone. He is trying to take Jenelle's life by having no friends and it's not going to work. It's none of his business or anything else what Jenelle does. I wrote on her wall—leave it, I want their friends and Bill to see what I said. I'm going to get after him if he don't stop running his fucking mouth, and Fuck Him. I know everything that's going on and I see and

*hear I'm not dumb like they think. They do need to leave you
all alone.*

*If I thought anything bad about Jamie I would have said
something and I have his back always he's a good guy and I
don't like a lot of people and you know this. I just pick good
people. And Bill knows who I am, what I look like and what I do
but he can't think of me LMAO fucker head. He just is trying to
make up all the lies he can and Lindsey ugly ass hooker fucker
face is just a Brat and ugly ... Billie Jean is a fucker head too. I
hate them all. I heard what Bill said tonight and let me tell you
something FUCK them ... We got Jamie's back and tell Jamie to
stay if he wants anytime because they are after him a lot, and
no need of this fucking shit. We are pissed off guys. We will be
around. Happy you made it home safe. I will talk to you soon.*

Love, your son Chris
God Bless

Buddy took the threats and harassment seriously, and he
began sitting up all night long to watch over Barbara and
Jenelle. As Barbara, Chris, Buddy, and Jamie talked about
what needed to be done, it became increasingly clear that
there was only one solution. The local police—idiots, the
family said—had repeatedly refused to help and were
taking the side of the people who had lived in town longer.
They were never going to stop, unless they were *made* to
stop.

Jamie felt comforted by the fact that Chris had his back,
as well as by the fact that Buddy, a former marine, was also
CIA. When Jamie inherited an AK-47 from his late brother,
Buddy had taken him out for some "training" and taught
him all about shooting and cleaning guns. He really seemed
to know what he was doing.

The family had dinner together, all agreeing that

Barbara's pineapple upside-down cake was delicious. Jenelle had progressed to secretly sending nude selfies to Jamie and assured him that, one day, they would elope. Jamie forwarded those selfies to his own email account, carefully labeling each one, so that he could enjoy them over and over.

Chris even gave Jamie advice on romancing Jenelle. He told her he should take her out to dinner, give her a card, light candles and "make the bed really pretty and just love on her." Jamie was keen, but the risk of getting caught sneaking her out of the house was just too great.

On December 14, 2011, Jamie offered clean Barbara's computer of files that he said were slowing her computer down, and assured her that Bill, Billie, and Lindsey "will get what's coming to them."

Jenelle wrote to Jamie on January 9, 2012:

Hey baby

I love you so much and I thank you for everything you have done for me and given me. You are the very best and You're not just my best friend but you are the love of my life and ever will be. You're my Husband and You will always be in my life and You make me so happy and smile so much and I can't see my life without you and I just wanted to let you know you are my everything and you mean the world to me. You are truly my other half and my heart and so much more. There will never be a day that goes by

I will love you more and more. You're awesome and you're my soul and heart. I love you sooo much. You are loved and needed and wanted. You're just my life. I hope you know all of this. But in case you didn't, you know now.

I will always be in your life and I will always Love you and be in love with you and need you. Your not just a part of me you are all of me. I love you so much baby.

Your wife
Jenelle

A couple of weeks later, Roy and Linda Stephens went to collect their mail from Paw Bill and made their grisly discovery.

13

SUSPECTS AND INTERVIEWS

I love to dance and love music. I like to write a lot and watch movies. I love to SHOOT GUNS for fun and no, not at anyone. Just not to be afraid to Enjoy every second that your alive. I love to live life. If you dont you might miss something so great b/c you are scared. Love life and God. and things will be great. :)

— JENELLE'S MYSPACE INTRODUCTION

The double murder was the biggest incident Johnson County had seen in a very long time. It dominated the news that night. The TV stations all ran with the same photograph, obtained from Paw Bill, of the couple posing proudly with their new baby. Everyone in town knew the couple, or at least members of their families, and everyone had their own theories about who was responsible. That evening, members of Billie Jean's family appeared on the news, begging the person who killed the young parents to come forward and confess.

Billie Jean's older sister, Beverley, said tearfully, "She was such a happy person, such a happy mom. I don't know why they would do this to her. I don't understand ... please come forward and confess to this, because this ain't fair. This ain't right." She pointed to baby Tyler being carried by another family member. "This ain't fair to him to lose his mom and dad."

Billie Jean's mother, Martha, said, "Having to leave the six-month-old baby with no daddy and no mommy and she loved this baby, both of them did, to death ... I didn't know a soul that didn't like them."

Despite Billie Jean's mother not knowing anyone who disliked her daughter and son-in-law, once the police started their investigation and began making their enquiries, friends of Bill and Billie Jean kept repeating the same name. It was the name of the one family that both victims had conflicts with. The name "Potter" went straight to the top of Agent Lott's priority list, along with Bill Payne's cousin, Jamie Curd.

On February 2, 2012, Chief Deputy Woodard and Agent Lott knocked on the Potters' door. When a tall, young woman answered, the agent identified himself: "Scott Lott with the Tennessee Bureau of Investigations."

Jenelle responded in her high-pitched, girlish voice, "Oh, OK, nice to meet you." She let him into the house, the front door opening directly into the living room, where her parents, Buddy and Barbara, were sitting. Woodard explained they were investigating a double homicide.

Buddy was immediately defensive. "Everybody always points the finger at us," he said. "I'm sorry that those people died, I don't wish that on nobody. You know me, I've been up there—oh I don't know how many times—because of them, I just don't wish that on nobody, though. When we saw that yesterday afternoon on the

TV, I mean ... that was a shock to see that that had happened."

Agent Lott assured them that nobody was pointing fingers, then asked, "Do you know of anybody who would want to hurt them?"

Jenelle answered. "No, actually, I don't, and I feel bad about this situation because I didn't want no harm on them. They've been harassing me on our driveway and on our property. And then, yesterday morning, when I got on Facebook is when I found out. And um, I mean ... I'm sorry it happened, but I mean that's all I can tell you is that they ... they had been harassing the living crap outta me."

The agents asked her why they would have been targeting her, and Jenelle's response surprised them. She said: "It came out to be a jealousy thing. They said I was too pretty, that I wasn't from around here and would never be accepted." This seemed like an absurd observation, given that Billie Jean was considered around town to be quite the beauty, whereas Jenelle was plain at best.

Jenelle was eager to talk to the police. She described how she had met Bill through his sister, Tracy, but that she felt uncomfortable after attending a party at Paw Bill's where drinking, drug use, and weapons, including an AK-47, were present. After that Jenelle told Tracy that she would never go to another party with her. Her real problems with Bill and Billie Jean, she said, began when their friend, Lindsey Thomas, abused her at the grocery store for using food stamps. She said that, after that incident, they created fake Facebook accounts using her picture, hacked into her social media accounts, and continually harassed her and threatened to have her raped. She claimed that her enemies would kill her parents to get to her. She said that Bill Payne had shot at her house, resulting in her going to hospital.

Barbara jumped in to confirm her daughter's version of events, adding, "They hacked in and threatened Jenelle, saying 'We want you dead'." Barbara said that Buddy caught Jenelle's tormentors trying to put sugar in the Potters' gas tanks, that they scratched Buddy's truck, broke their garage door, and threw rocks at the house and Jenelle's window.

Jenelle denied ever posting anything negative or inflammatory on the internet about the victims and stated that she had only asked her tormentors to leave her alone. When asked if she had wished the victims dead online, Jenelle responded, "No, no. I'm not that mean."

Jenelle also claimed that Bill had publicly accused both Buddy and Jamie of selling drugs, which was completely untrue. In fact, Jenelle was sure it was Bill and Billie Jean who sold drugs. She said she felt in jeopardy all the time, even when going out with her parents, because the group had threatened to kill Buddy and Barbara to get to Jenelle. She said, "Bill was always trying to push someone's buttons."

Seizing on the name "Jamie," another person on their radar, the detective asked, "What's Jamie to you?"

Jenelle responded, "He's just a friend. We've been friends for years." The detectives noted that the whole family seemed to be on the defensive, with Barbara and Buddy insisting that Jamie was only a family friend and definitely *not* Jenelle's boyfriend, nor did he want to be. Jenelle told the police officers that Bill and Jamie had recently had a falling out due to Jamie supporting Jenelle during the recent phone harassment case.

When Agent Lott asked Jenelle who she thought might have committed the crime, she implied that the couple had many enemies, saying that anyone who came into contact with the victims had trouble with them. She insisted that she would never be able to do it, never be able to hurt anyone; that is, unless they were going to rape her.

As they finished up, Buddy reassured the officers, in no uncertain terms, that despite all the threats and harassment, he would never wish murder upon anybody.

"Especially with a baby," added Jenelle.

14

MOTIVES AND ARRESTS

I have the best Momma and Daddy in the world. They have really been there for me and they are great people. My Daddy was in the Marines and him and my mom were married while he was in the Marines. He was in Vietnam and my mom was working and they were married when they both were 18 and 19 years old. They have been together since they were 11 years old. Its so great. I love how they are and they have been through so much, but they are wonderful. I'm so lucky I am blessed with them.

— JENELLE'S MYSPACE INTRODUCTION

After visiting the Potters, the police were convinced they had what sounded like a pretty clear motive, though it had yet to be backed up by evidence. The Potters remained at the top of their list of suspects. They knew that Buddy always carried a gun, and they had seen evidence of many more firearms around the family home. However, in rural Tennessee, this was far from out of the ordinary. Plus, if Buddy was guilty, he would almost certainly have disposed of the murder weapon right after the act.

As news spread around Mountain City, fueled by social media, that the Potters may have had something to do with the murders, it didn't take long before early news reports began stating that the feud originated with the victims unfriending Jenelle on Facebook. The media were quick to latch onto this piece of information, dubbing it the "Facebook Unfriending" case.

Meanwhile, a few days after the homicides, JD Weinberger reported that Buddy and Jenelle shopped at his Food Lion store, and that they had mentioned the murders to him. When JD expressed sympathy for the victims and said he didn't know how someone could commit the crimes while Billie Jean held her child, Buddy and Jenelle glared at him. While subsequently describing that interaction, he told folks, "If looks could kill, I'd have been dead then."

Police recognized that they weren't exactly dealing with criminal masterminds. They called Jamie in for a second interview, having had him come to the station the first time soon after the discovery of the bodies. He slumped in the chair, ready to provide monosyllabic responses to their questions again.

This time, he was asked to take a polygraph test. Although such tests are notoriously unreliable and therefore not admissible in court, police often find them useful in interrogations to discover how people act when they are telling lies. The test told them that Jamie was not being honest with them, particularly when asked whether he knew who killed Bill and Billie Jean.

The interrogators relayed the results to Jamie and assured him, "We're not looking to crucify anybody. We just want the truth. We're looking for who pulled the trigger, that's all." Their grilling of Jamie so far had also given them some insight as to what kind of man he was, and their questioning exploited that. "Are you the type of man who could shoot a woman, probably begging for her life, while her baby is in her arms?"

Jamie responded, "No."

The detective agreed, "No, you couldn't do that. But you know who did, don't you? Your eyes are a window to your soul. I can see your soul, and I'm looking right into your soul." He appealed to Jamie's better nature, telling him how much better he would feel if he would only tell the truth. Jamie's denials became less convincing, his demeanor more agitated.

After about an hour and a half of interrogation, sensing that Jamie was beginning to crack, the officers leaned in and pressed him. "Who shot him? Who had the gun?"

Jamie responded, "He did"

They kept pushing. "He who? Buddy?"

"Yeah," Jamie said.

As he prepared to tell them all about that fateful night, Jamie said, "There's one question you didn't answer me, that's been blowing in the wind. Is the CIA here?"

When they asked incredulously why he wanted to know about the CIA, Jamie explained it was because Buddy had told him he was with the secretive agency. He told investigators he participated in the murders because he was afraid of Buddy and believed that the murders had been ordered by the US Government. He stated that he had not wanted to kill anyone, had never done anything violent before, felt horrible about the murders, and that he considered Bill to be like a brother. "I was hoping the CIA had my back," Jamie said.

The investigating officers were dumbfounded.

It had been a long, hard interrogation and it was easing into the early hours of February 7 when Agent Lott asked Jamie to call Buddy. He instructed Jamie to ask the older man what he had done with the gun and knife used during the murders, so they could capture the response on tape.

Barbara answered the phone and spoke with Jamie for a few minutes. She told him that Chris had sent an email to her, indicating that Jamie had been arrested. She asked Jamie if he had taken a lie detector test and then whether he had passed it. He said yes to both questions. When Buddy came to the phone, Jamie muttered down the line, "Well, they're pointin' fingers."

"Oh, Jiminy Christmas!" Buddy responded. He told Jamie that there was no reason for anyone to point fingers at him, because Bill was involved in drugs and that the homicides looked like a "drug deal gone bad."

As instructed by the cops, Jamie said, "You got rid of everything that was from Bill's, right?"

"Uh-huh," Buddy responded.

"OK, that makes me feel a lot better," Jamie said.

Buddy's replies were kept short. "Yeah."

It was not quite a smoking gun, but the phone call was enough for investigators to obtain a warrant for Buddy Potter's arrest, and a search warrant for his home and truck that same morning.

Police descended on the Potter residence in the early hours of Tuesday, February 7, 2012, and arrested Buddy who, as usual, was armed, even at 3:30 a.m. They took him down hard when he reached down to pull his gun from its holster, then a crew of officers went through the house methodically, searching for anything that might be used as evidence against him. Any items of interest were brought to Chief Deputy Woodard so that he could determine whether it should be logged, bagged, and removed from the premises.

Barbara and Jenelle sat side-by-side on a couch in the living room across from Woodard as police tore through the house, bagging, tagging, and removing anything that could be related to the crimes. Woodard was surprised when Barbara reached for a stack of papers that were awaiting his inspection and began frantically ripping them in half. All this did was draw attention to the items she was trying to destroy. Woodard promptly demanded she hand them over.

The stack of papers consisted of emails printed on inkjet printer, including screenshots of several photographs apparently lifted from Facebook. The photographs were of Jenelle's sworn enemies—Lindsey Thomas and Billie Jean Hayworth. Some were of the girls in skimpy "saucy school-girl" costumes and others in swimwear. The emails had subject lines like "Billie Whore" for Billie Jean and "Pan-face" for Lindsey. Woodard decided that these papers did, indeed, bear some relation to the murders and had them taken in as evidence.

This wasn't the only interesting stack of paper detectives found. In the back of Buddy's truck they discovered three large garbage bags full of shredded paper, bundled up as if ready to be disposed of. They took those bags away too.

Officers seized the one computer that was clearly shared by the family, an external hard drive, and a handy green spiral notebook on a desk next to the computer monitor, which contained passwords to various internet accounts, including passwords for both Jenelle's and Barbara's email accounts.

They also seized what detectives later called "an arse-nal," consisting of thirty-two firearms in total, including rifles, semi-automatics, handguns, an AK-47, and various shotguns, along with a huge supply of ammunition. Every corner of the house seemed to have some sort of weapon stashed away. Some were standing up against walls, others were tucked in drawers or hung from the antlers of hunting trophies. Buddy's truck was impounded, and everything was sent to the TBI crime lab for testing. Buddy was made to accompany the officers back to the police station. He was given no time to gather his thoughts before being led into the same interrogation room Jamie had sat in earlier, and asked, "You know why you're here, right?"

He responded, "That someone told you that I'm the one that killed somebody." Sitting uncomfortably in jeans and a red sweater, clutching his water bottle, Buddy proceeded to deny everything. But the seasoned detectives knew which buttons to press. They already knew Buddy from his many calls and visits to the police station and doubted that this puffy bozo was really a CIA operative. They knew he was devoted to his wife and daughter and demanded to know, "A cold-hearted killer, or protector of your family? Which one are you?"

Buddy responded, "I'm a protector of my family to start with, but I did not do this."

Agent Lott kept pressing. "I believe that you are sick and tired that the most precious person in your life is being attacked and harassed constantly." They told him they thought that he had been convinced to carry out the dastardly deed by Jamie, who wanted to prove that he was good enough to take care of Jenelle. Buddy was having none of it. He didn't believe that the family friend wanted to be Jenelle's boyfriend, and even if he did, he was adamant that Jenelle wasn't interested in Jamie in that way.

They told him that Jamie had already implicated him, to which Buddy whined, "He's throwing me under the bus."

As the hours wore on, Buddy appeared to get emotional, shaking his head from side to side, his voice becoming husky. He began to open up about the trauma he and his family had endured and the constant danger that lurked around every corner. Buddy said there was a $3,000 bounty on his, Barbara's, and Jenelle's heads. "Ever since all this crap started, I've been ... I've had my life threatened, my wife has been threatened, they've threatened to take Jenelle, cut her head off ..." He choked up, on the verge of tears. "When you hear people plottin' to catch your daughter in a restroom and murder her ... they wanted to rape her because she's a virgin and just ... so much *bullshit!*"

As Buddy sobbed silently, a detective asked, "Do Jenelle and Barbara know what you did?"

"No," said Buddy firmly.

Once they had as much as they thought they could get out of Buddy that morning, they suggested that he be the one to tell his wife what he had done. With the tape once again recording, Buddy called Barbara. "Barbara, before you find out from somebody else, I want you to know. I was involved in it. I did it ... I ... I didn't want you to be afraid no more."

Rather than sounding shocked, Barbara responded calmly that he could not have committed the crimes because "I saw you sittin' there" at home at the time of the murders. She repeated this to him, insisting that he had been there with her the whole time. "I saw you," she said.

"I love you. I did it to protect you," Buddy insisted. But Barbara wasn't having it.

She said, "You're not guilty because you were here. You have to say that. You were here. I saw you ... you haven't had no rest, and you don't have your oxygen, and you're not yourself right now." Before concluding the call, Barbara repeated her mantra. "Don't worry, honey. You were right here. I saw you right here."

Detectives were mystified. Was this merely a loving wife trying to provide an alibi for her husband, or something more?

15

MURDERERS BEHIND BARS

L ater, Barbara accused the police of taking Buddy and interviewing him for hours without allowing him access to the oxygen he needed to function. She said they'd coerced a confession out of him when he was unable to breathe properly and that when he was denied his oxygen he often said strange and untrue things. But, in the meantime, on February 8, Jamie Curd and Buddy Potter were charged with first-degree murder. Detectives began gathering the evidence they needed for a conviction. Special Agent Miranda Gaddes was given the unenviable task of piecing together the paper found in the garbage bags in the back of Buddy's truck, shred by shred. It was a painstakingly slow process, but investigators were sure that, if the Potters had wanted whatever it was gone so badly, it most likely held one of the many keys to this case.

With both Buddy and Jamie in prison, Jenelle tapped out a series of texts to her online friend, Melanie, telling her about the arrests of her father and boyfriend. "They think they killed Bill and Billie," she wrote, "This has got me and my mom so upset. I think they got Jamie. His cell phone is off and house phone just rings. I don't understand." In further messages, Jenelle said, "I wish I knew what Jamie is thinking. It's bad -- the whole -- the town is being really evil" and asked, "Do you think Jamie still loves me? I just hope Jamie don't hate me."

Melanie was confused. Why wouldn't Jamie still love Jenelle? After all, Jenelle hadn't committed any crime, had she? Wasn't she the innocent bystander in all of this?

As investigators delved further into the family, it emerged that the real reason that the Potters had moved from Pennsylvania to Mountain City was that Buddy Potter had been found guilty of stolen valor - lying about the extent of his military service. Although it was true that he had been in the Marines, rather than being part of a pilot rescue team, his primary job was gathering supply parts for helicopters. He had never won the medals or accolades that he claimed, nor had he ever been on the tours he said he'd been on. The photos he so proudly displayed were frauds. He had altered his Department of the Navy letter and discharge certificate to include medals he'd never earned, and additional training that he'd never had.

Buddy had walked into court to face the charges "hunched over, grimacing in pain, with the aid of a cane; rolling a portable oxygen bottle in front of him." The judge reportedly sentenced Buddy to six months' probation and ordered forfeiture of all unauthorized medals and awards. Buddy also had to write a letter to the President of Vietnam Veterans of America and pay a $500 fine. Judge Smith felt that "this sentence was appropriate considering the health and financial condition of the Defendant." It is not clear whether Barbara and Jenelle were aware of this, but Buddy Potter had left Pennsylvania in deep disgrace.

News of Jamie and Buddy being arrested, and their

confessions, spread around the small community like wild-fire, and, as always, Topix was the hub of the gossip. The more salacious news services had run with the narrative that it all stemmed from Jenelle Potter being unfriended on Facebook by the victims, although the truth was clearly much more complicated than that.

The Topix thread called "Jenelle Potter strikes again" was revived. Jerseydevil wrote: *This whole thing sounds like a Lifetime movie plot. I mean, my gawd, he KILLED two people; left the baby splashing in mama's blood, because his grown-assed daughter had a riff on Facebook? It's just too nutty for me to wrap my head around.*

Astute contributors pointed to the obsessive feud as being indicative of a deeper problem in Mountain City—some people were just as addicted to social media as they were to drugs. Some craved the validation of online friends; others craved the drama it brought into their otherwise mundane lives, like the poster who clearly watched way too much TV, and who declared Paw Bill should be the primary suspect, and next should be the local state trooper, as he was most likely to be capable of carrying out what they described as "an execution-style murder."

With bonds set at $1.5 million each, it was unlikely either Buddy or Jamie would make bail. Jamie had quickly recanted his confession the day after he had made it. In one of his phone calls from the prison afterwards, according to the book *Too Pretty to Live* (written by the prosecutor of the case), he told a relative, "When that prosecutor comes and offers me a plea bargain, I'm gonna tell him to shove it up his ass." Jamie still felt close to the Potter family, and still hoped that his and Jenelle's relationship would continue despite the predicament he found himself in.

Jenelle, meanwhile, went about her life, only leaving the

house in the company of her mother to go shopping. On one such occasion, she was overheard in Fred's discount store asking the cashiers if they had seen her on TV. Soon, the posts on Topix began to question whether Jenelle had also been complicit in the murders.

As is often the case for overworked police departments and district attorneys, nothing moved as fast as the friends and family of the victims would have liked. In July 2012, local newspapers received a letter from David Garland, Bill Payne's stepfather, criticizing Johnson County Sheriff Mike Reece's handling of what had become known as "The Facebook Murders."

With the massive publicity the case had garnered, those who were not part of the local Facebook or Topix groups learned of the ongoing feud that had been simmering in Mountain City for years through the news. David Garland's letter drew attention to the fact that the sheriff's office had received numerous complaints from people about the Potter family. There had even been orders of protection filed against Janelle Potter, alleging online and telephone harassment that stretched back for at least four years. David Garland's letter said that, given this background information and the ongoing issues related to the Potter family, the sheriff should have done more to protect the two victims.

In the comments section of the Johnson County Press, someone wrote: *I dated [Buddy's] daughter a few years ago. She seemed to have some real mental problems and believed people were out to get her. Her dad would always walk around with a gun and even stated once that he sat in his driveway waiting for someone that was "harassing" his daughter to pull in so he could shoot them. He even bragged that he could do it and get away with it. I am not surprised when I found out he was charged with this.*

Someone else wrote: *What about the Potter girl? Shouldn't she also be charged along with her evil, horrible, waste of skin father? I bet she was the instigator in all this and, if she was, then she should face the same charges and also be slowly tortured to death. I do not think these people should have any food, water, or even a place to sleep. They should be tied and chained to a tree in the woods and let the animals have them.*

Not all wished quite as gruesome a fate on the family, but armchair lawyers and psychologists abounded, like the one who wrote: *The two men would never get off on insanity, but Janelle sure as hell might. Seems like she has multiple internet personalities, and likes to make up "friends" and then she uses multiple accounts to 'talk to herself' and agree with herself. Did this girl have ANY REAL friends? Did anyone on here know her personally, other than what they've been reading?*

It seemed everyone knew the Potter family was unhinged, but, even so, nobody really suspected that they would go so far as to commit murder over online insults.

16

A BAG FULL OF EMAILS

Happy Birthday! It is amazing that you & Jenelle were born on the same day, same year, 1 minute apart & at the same hospital! You're the same age too. Isn't that quite a coincidence?

— BARBARA POTTER'S FACEBOOK
MESSAGE TO CHRIS, APRIL 27, 2011

Special Agent Miranda Gaddes had done an incredible job of piecing together the shredded pages from the back of Buddy's truck. From the three large garbage bags, she had managed to reconstruct around 100 pages over several months. The results proved to be both enlightening and confounding to investigators.

In the reassembled documents, the author and recipient were not always specified. Many of the messages appeared to be between Barbara and a mysterious person called Chris, and, when read in context, some of the messages appeared to be reproductions of communications that originated from another account, such as Facebook, Myspace, or Topix.

The email messages were dated from January 2011 to January 25, 2012. Barbara referred to Chris as "son," although the police were not aware of the Potters having any children other than Jenelle and her estranged sister Christie. Chris and Barbara went into great detail to each other about the constant harassment of the Potter family, especially the suffering of Jenelle due to the harassment from the three girls, Lindsey, Tara, and Billie Jean, as well as from Bill. Both Chris and Barbara referred to the three women with decidedly disparaging language ("whore" being a particular favorite), and many of the messages included some sort of threat or desire for violence, harm, and even death to the group.

In one message, Chris told Barbara that she should be wary of her daughter, Christie, whom Chris declared "is after you all a lot. and after what i saw in the court room she wants you dead and out of the pictrue." He told Barbara that Chrisie was offering sex and blow jobs for money to all the guys around town, but that they turned her down, and that Barbara's mother, with whom Christie was living, was also not to be trusted.

Barbara frequently badgered Chris for Buddy's missing "CIA identification" that had apparently been promised to him for some time. There were things Buddy wanted to do, but he wanted to be sure he had the backing of the CIA before he did. Barbara apparently clung to the delusion that she was married to some sort of super-spy, despite the findings of the court in Pennsylvania that he lied about his service. Chris assured her the backing was there, even if the ID was tied up in some sort of bureaucratic red tape.

In one message from Barbara to Chris, dated April 5, 2011, she said that Jenelle's three main female tormentors "need to die!" In another message, Barbara urged Chris to "disable all of their vehicles" and asserted that "they have to go to prison or die." She seemed to have little doubt that the CIA had sent an operative to look out for the Potter family and be Jenelle's guardian angel, wiling to inflict vengeance on those who would do her harm. Six days before the murders, Chris referred to Lindsey as "whore Lindsey," before remarking that her birthday was coming up, and how he hoped that "she dies before then."

Reading these messages, Agent Lott decided the answer to what truly motivated these murders would be found in the Potters' computer, among their emails and social media. The green spiral notebook which neatly laid out the various usernames and passwords of the Potter women would come in handy for this purpose. Just to be on the safe side, as they suspected many of the communications might have been deleted, they also obtained subpoenas for permanent records from Yahoo and AOL. The resulting DVD they received contained over 20,000 emails. Among them, besides the weird communications from Chris, something else stood out. In mid-January, Barbara had sent herself two links: "Christian News: Can God Forgive a Murderer?" and "Billy Graham—questions about forgiveness & murder."

Why would Barbara, whom Buddy had sworn knew nothing about his plans to kill Bill and Billie Jean, be wondering if God could forgive murderers two weeks before the murders were carried out?

17

CHRIS FROM THE CIA

Then I have Chris. I have known him for a very long, long time. He's a cop in PA. He's a good guy and a true friend and almost like a Brother to me and married to a wonderful girl named Megan. I wish nothing but the best for you both.

— JENELLE'S MYSPACE INTRODUCTION

P art of the investigation team's intent was to uncover who the mysterious "Chris" really was. The emails between Barbara and Chris began on January 1, 2011. The first email he wrote said: *Hi Barbara. How are you? I hope you are well. Yes this is Chris A.K.A. Cody. I'm so sorry to hear all of that is going on. I wish there was a way to help you all. I can't come up there and see you—if someone saw me it would not be a good thing. I hope to get out and talk though. I ran by Topix because I saw that they said Jenelle was up here and with Buddy and you, and I saw it and got on there and I took care of it. They were doing nothing about it.*

He went on to tell Barbara about his work with the CIA, claiming that he'd shot many people in the line of duty and had "gotten rid of" people in Russia and New York. "I got to a point where they were bad people and I knew it was us or them, so I had to kill," he wrote. "But I love to shoot now. And killing does not bother me at all."

Through a series of messages back and forth, Barbara let him know, "As long as you are doing the right thing for mankind, then you will not be judged badly. If it is like Buddy did, you are helping others by getting rid of the bad." Buddy had regaled Barbara with several tales involving his supposed "license to kill" while he was in the CIA, and Barbara had hung on every word.

Chris assured Barbara that he could kill her daughter, Christie, and other family members in Pennsylvania, saying that now that he had them in his sights, he could get to them anytime, which, he said, "I just might." He warned her that she was not safe, and that Christie was dangerous, telling Barbara that she should not go to her mother's house alone, before signing off with, "I love you all, your son, Chris."

As the months passed, discussion of the conflict between Barbara and her mother and daughter diminished, and the focus of the messages became Bill, Billie Jean and Lindsey. Throughout the chain of emails, Chris shared information about his work with the CIA and referred to the local Johnson County law enforcement as "dumb and untrustworthy." He seemed to know the names of many local police officers, who he didn't hesitate to deem incompetent and ineffective. He wrote about his intervention in the harassment by the "mean girls" and how he defended Jenelle, whom he described as a "good person" and as "trying to make peace."

Barbara would, from time to time, try to arrange a meeting with Chris, suggesting Buddy could meet him in the CIA building and then bring him downstairs to secretly meet with Barbara and Jenelle, who would be sitting in the back seat of the truck where the windows were blacked out. He just had to say the word and she would pass the message on to Buddy. She also assured him that if "they" killed her, Buddy would "do what he was trained to do." She began to sign her messages to Chris as "Mom Barbie".

Barbara also shared her desire for Jenelle to have someone to "take care of her and be good to her," but left him with no doubt that the person for the job was definitely not Jamie. One message to Chris read, in part: *These guys down here are trash and we threw the last one out last year in January—jerk Jamie Curd. He took advantage of me, & was dirty, muddy, and walked in the house any old time, even when Jen was in the hospital one time! He did not have good manners and smelled, too. He used to hang out with Bill Payne, the "maybe" father of Billie Jean Hayworth's baby, not sure yet, and he is running a whore house you know. We would not let her go out in the car with him because he had a trap for a car and we did not trust him. She did not want to go out with him either. She is such a good person.*

Barbara sent several emails to Chris about her dislike of Jamie, regaling him with the story of Jenelle running away to be with him and boasting that she and Buddy made sure that there would be no romance there. She wrote: *It took some rough treatment for us to get rid of him; he wouldn't stop! Finally by end of March, told him off good, Bud warned him for the last time, and it's over. The guys down here are basically no good ... and she has finally found out. I don't know much about him, but he lives back in the holler. Jen would not survive long over there with his old grouchy sick mom. She would have been alone most of time, tried to be a nurse for mom. But! She was so sorry she did that; he had her brainwashed & so scared & mixed up.*

Chris's emails to Barbara remained focused mostly on Jenelle's tormentors, but he also took great care to defend Jamie, saying that he had kept an eye on him and had discovered that he was no longer friendly with his cousin Bill. Chris had set Jamie a test, and Jamie had passed, telling Chris everything he knew about Bill. Chris therefore thought Barbara should give Jamie another chance. But Barbara remained unmoved, saying "Jamie is not welcome here ever again."

When she wrote about the harassment Jenelle was suffering at the hands of the "mean girls" who constantly "hacked" Jenelle's social media, Barbara became incoherent. She badgered Chris to talk to his superiors to have Buddy's CIA identification reissued and to get him reactivated so that he could get access to "CIA guns." Chris assured her he was already on it, that the CIA knew about Buddy, and that he could be called up at any time. "We need all the CIA we can get to do a job," he wrote. The "job" that the CIA was primarily focused on, according to Chris, was protecting the Potter family from their tormentors, most notably Billie Jean Hayworth, Lindsey Thomas, and Bill Payne.

As Buddy didn't use a computer, Barbara printed out any important information from Chris, passed it on to Buddy, and then shredded the paper once he had been brought up to date. She referred to Buddy as "a sharpshooter & sniper" and hinted he was standing by to be deployed and to commit acts of violence against people in Mountain City. "He'd really like to be involved in a lot of things, especially Christie, cuffing her when the time comes, etc," Barbara wrote. Christie was Buddy's own daughter.

The emails became warmer and more familiar between Barbara and Chris as time went on, though they both also grew increasingly angry and hysterical about the treatment of Jenelle and, by extension, the Potter family, by the "mean girls" in town. Barbara wrote to him: "You are welcome to shoot any of them but let Christie's body be found—we have life insurance on her so may as well collect it ... I know that sounds mean for a mom to say, but she hates me, wants me dead as well as dad & Jen."

Barbara Potter was apparently trying to take out a hit on her own daughter and was joking—or possibly not joking at all—about collecting the life insurance. "if someone wants to bring it on, they will all die, including the baby," Barbara wrote in another email. "We want peace and no one here wants to kill anyone, but we will." She said she no longer bothered calling 911, because the police were useless, but that she would do whatever she had to do to save Jenelle or herself. She wrote that "we are ready to take care of this ourselves," and compared herself to a mother lion, writing "I'll do whatever it takes to save my young! I will kill if I have to, not just hurt but kill."

Chris fed into Barbara's growing bloodlust and quest for vengeance over perceived slights directed at Jenelle. He assured her that he was keen to kill them all—Mike Reece, the Johnson County Sheriff, then Lindsey, followed by Billie Jean and Bill. However, he always supplied reasons why he couldn't carry out the slayings himself. He assured her that, if Buddy decided to take matters into his own hands, he would be protected. Buddy was "in the computer as CIA, and that's all that matters."

The emails confused investigators. On the one hand, they were 100 per cent sure that "Chris" was not CIA or a law enforcement officer of any kind. It was extremely unlikely a CIA operative would ever write something like

"I'm going to run into whore pan slut face ugly as a mudd face bitch and her fucker of a BF," or would take an intense interest in such an ordinary family as the Potters. It seemed that all his emails, to both Jamie and Barbara, came via Jenelle's email account. But Barbara referred to him as "her son" despite there being no evidence that she had a son. Jenelle said that he was "like a brother" to her. Detectives knew that Chris certainly wasn't who he appeared to be.

Jenelle's Myspace introduction included a reference to Chris being some kind of law enforcement personnel in Pennsylvania. Some of the email messages the investigators had recovered contained photographs of Chris, his dog, and his friends. One message from Barbara's account had the subject line "Pic of CHRIS, our son." This email contained text that read, "this is Chris Tjaden back at youth camp, with Jenelle—age 18 or so (our son)," along with a blurry photograph of two people wearing what appeared to be military fatigues.

In one of her private Facebook messages, Barbara had written to a friend, claiming Chris Tjaden had helped Jenelle fight off bullies at school. Barbara called Chris her adopted son, and said that the family loved him, but didn't get to see him often enough.

It was time to contact Chris Tjaden and find out what was really going on.

Christopher Tjaden worked as a certified constable in Wilmington, Delaware, and had previously worked for the Delaware City Police Department. He came from a law enforcement family; his father was chief of police in a small city. Chris had a reasonably active Facebook profile, and it didn't take investigators long to track him down.

The young man told detectives it was true he had attended high school with Jenelle, whom he recalled as being "very strange." Chris, who was popular and successful at school, said that he had two classes with Jenelle, and spoke to her occasionally, but that they weren't part of the same social group. If he was nice to her, she sometimes hung around, as though she wanted to be friends, but he extricated himself politely. She was known to throw tantrums and had problems with many of her classmates, and she was in trouble a lot. Like most people, he did his best to keep his distance from her. He certainly never drove her to school or waited for her after track practice, as she had claimed.

Chris was surprised to hear that Jenelle and Barbara considered him to be "like family," as not only had he not given Jenelle Potter a second thought after graduation, but he had also never even met Buddy or Barbara. He didn't know the name Jamie Curd, and he had never served in the CIA.

Chris identified himself in four photos shown to him by the investigators, including one sent from Jenelle's email account to Jamie with the subject line, "My Chris." He said that while the photographs of him at a baseball game and standing next to his patrol car had both previously been used as profile pictures on his Facebook, he and Jenelle were not connected as Facebook friends. She had sent him a friend request once, which he initially accepted, but when he checked her page and saw nothing but crazy religious ramblings interspersed by pictures of bulldogs, he immediately unfriended her again. However, his past and present profile photographs were available for any Facebook user to access and download, whether or not they were friends.

Agent Lott showed him several more photos that had been sent from both Barbara's and Jenelle's email accounts to Jamie Curd, purporting to be Chris, but he didn't recognize them at all. Some photographs were simply of men who bore some resemblance or were so blurry that the men in them could pass as him. He didn't recognize a dog that was in a photograph tagged "chris's dog Little maggie," nor a red Ferrari in another picture. Another photograph purported to be Chris' wife and her brother, but he didn't recognize either of the people.

It didn't take long for Agent Lott to rule out the perplexed, happily married man as having written the emails and social media messages that had apparently come from Chris. The revelation didn't come as a surprise, as whoever wrote the messages from Chris used not only Jenelle's email account to send them, but also had an almost identical style of writing to Jenelle. There was just one major difference—Jenelle never cussed, and Chris used foul language all the time. As they started digging deeper, investigators formed the opinion that Jenelle and Chris were one and the same person.

It was not beyond reason that the dimwitted Jamie had not caught on to the deception. But why would Barbara believe the messages from Chris? Why would she call the man she had never met "son" and refer to herself as "Mom Barbie"?

The answer might lie in the internet phenomenon of "catfishing."

"Catfishing" refers to using a fake internet persona to form a relationship with someone under false pretenses. It is sometimes used to fool people into sending money to someone they believe has a romantic interest in them, and who is often far more attractive than the victim's usual partners. Catfishers may simply want to string someone along, embarrass them, or trick them into providing information that they would not otherwise divulge. Usually, the catfisher does not even know the person they are fooling, but sometimes it is someone known to the victim, using a fake name, photograph, and personal information.

Could the big, bullied, simple Jenelle be catfishing both her boyfriend and her own mother?

Investigators knew that if they could just convince Jamie that Chris had never existed, he might turn state's evidence against Buddy Potter. However, Jamie remained steadfast. He loved his girlfriend and he might finally have the approval of her parents. He'd lost his own mother, father, and a brother. No way was he going to turn on his new family.

18

MOUNTAIN CITY VS THE POTTERS

Billy Ray Payne, age 58, of Mountain City, Tennessee, passed away from a broken heart

— OBITUARY FOR BILLY RAY "PAW BILL"
PAYNE, APRIL 18, 2013

On April 18, 2013, Paw Bill died at just 58 years of age, before he could see justice done for the murder of his son and daughter-in-law. Tributes for Paw Bill flowed in from friends, neighbors, and work-mates, all calling him gentle, easygoing, a man who would do anything for his family, a man who was overjoyed that they had lived with him to bring up the baby. Many agreed that Paw Bill did, indeed, die of a broken heart.

A few weeks later, emergency services received a call from Barbara Potter asking police to come to the Mountain City Pharmacy "to help get us out safely." She claimed she had been shopping with Jenelle when a woman came in threatening to attack them as soon as they left the store. When local police officers arrived, the woman in question

said that she had wanted to use the bathroom but feared
Jenelle and so she had left and waited outside. After
reviewing the CCTV tape and finding nothing untoward, the
police escorted Jenelle and Barbara to their car, and they left
without incident.

However, after that, Jenelle claimed she was the target of
ongoing threats and harassment from several local people
who she said blamed her for killing Paw Bill, a beloved
member of the community. Jenelle said they texted her,
called her, and even attacked her home. She insisted that
they "broke into my phone," which was something Jenelle
often claimed—that hackers left messages to make her look
like she was the one doing the harassing. Right after the
murders she had told police, "They were on my account.
They hacked in." Her mother had confirmed this. "They
hacked in all the time."

Meanwhile, it seemed like some people simply couldn't
keep away from the social media drama that was continuing
to fester in Mountain City. The Topix thread "Jenelle Potter
Strikes Again," was particularly hot. As people gossiped
about the Potters, new people kept on chiming in—people
who had a remarkably similar style of writing, and who
made the same errors in grammar, spelling, and punctuation as Jenelle Potter did. For example, someone called
"Jilly" ranted about how "sweet and caring" Jenelle was and
how the town had got it all wrong. She wrote, "Her sister is
in on this, and Lindsey Thomas, and her dumb little fucking
druggie friends."

About the murders, Jilly said, "It's a Drug Deal that went
Wrong. Can't anyone see this? Well Small towns come with
small Brains ..."

Other usernames that agreed with Jilly also took great
care to point out how "sweet and caring" Jenelle was and

what "mean girls" Billie Jean and her friends were. However, they were mostly drowned out by the sheer number of posters who believed that Jenelle Potter was complicit, and possibly just as guilty, as her father and boyfriend in the murders of Bill and Billie Jean. One wrote, "Jenelle, you're crazy. Guess what, I WAS your Facebook friend and defriended your psycho ass, I absolutely know this is you based upon your stupid comment and your lack of spelling/grammar skills. You need to stop lying to yourself and others. We all know it wasn't a drug deal, your freaking dad & loverboy confessed. Hell, I could've told you who killed them just by being your Facebook friend, how many posts did you make whining about those poor 2 innocent people that you harassed constantly? Get it through your thick skull, you are a horrible person. Accept what you've done to everyone's lives around you & get out of your fantasy world. Or better yet, just check yourself into a mental ward, and save the rest of society from your evilness."

The people of Mountain City - at least those who contributed to Topix - wanted Jenelle Potter to pay.

The sentiment running through local social media that Jenelle Potter was somehow responsible for the deaths of Bill and Billie Jean had not gone unnoticed. Carter County Assistant District Attorney Dennis Brooks had been reviewing all the evidence, including the mountains of email correspondence between Jenelle, Barbara, and Jamie. He reached the conclusion that it was not just Buddy and Jamie who were guilty of murder. Brooks believed there was enough in those communications to convince a grand jury that Barbara and Jenelle had both played active roles in inciting the homicides, and that they had deliberately targeted Jamie Curd to carry out the deed.

ADA Brooks noticed in particular that, as time went on,

Barbara seemed to hope that Chris would assassinate all the Potter family's enemies, but he always had an excuse for why he couldn't. The psychotic CIA agent suggested that if Buddy were to carry out the murders instead, then Chris and the CIA would have his back. As their emails progressed, Barbara grew worried that Buddy, with his disabilities, could not kill the younger, fitter tormentors on his own. Chris pointed out that there was one other person in Mountain City who cared enough about Jenelle to help Buddy: Jamie Curd. After that, Barbara warmed up to Jamie, inviting him into the family and beginning her own correspondence with him.

ADA Brooks was certain that Jenelle Potter was the mysterious CIA agent who called himself Chris. As Chris, and with her mother's help, she had convinced her gullible father and naïve boyfriend to murder her enemies. Not only that, but she had also written many of the social media posts, as well as the emails she forwarded to her mother, claiming Lindsey had sent them to her. Jenelle was nothing if not prolific in written communications.

On August 9, 2013, ADA Brooks accompanied Agent Lott and two other police officers to Johnston Memorial Hospital in Abingdon, Virginia, where Jenelle had been hospitalized for one of her many ailments. There, both Jenelle and Barbara were placed under arrest. According to Brooks's recounting of the event in his book *Too Pretty to Live*, Barbara's daughter Christie was on duty with the EMS at the hospital that day. Barbara, in handcuffs, spotted her daughter and allegedly "muttered something in [Christie's] direction, effectively attributing this new development to her."

Barbara and Jenelle were charged with two counts of first-degree murder and conspiracy to commit first-degree murder. Jamie was re-indicted to be tried in the same trial as they were. Buddy, the active shooter, was to be tried separately. ADA Brooks had a massive task to convince a jury that all four defendants should be held responsible for the deaths of Bill and Billie-Jean.

19

THE FIRST TRIAL

Buddy Potter's trial began in early October 2013.

Assistant District Attorney Dennis Brooks set the scene of the gruesome discovery by describing the neighbors stumbling upon the bodies and depicting the horrifying scene of a baby laying in his dead mother's arms. He described Buddy as someone "who was cold enough, calculating enough, and trained enough to be able to conduct murders like that," before saying, "At least, he thinks he is ... he likes to tell people he's that kind of person. He likes for his family to think he's that kind of person." The ADA described the bizarre social media situation that surrounded Buddy's daughter, and which eventually encompassed his entire family, his bragging about being in the CIA and his hold over his daughter's boyfriend, Jamie Curd.

For his part, the defense attorney, Randy Fallin, claimed the interrogation and subsequent confession of his client had been flawed and unfair, and was therefore inadmissible. His reasoning for this was that interrogators had denied Buddy his oxygen, causing an impaired mental state that led to strange, illogical statements. He pointed out that there had been methamphetamine laid out in Paw Bill's house, but that the victims had not tested positive to the drug, leading to a theory that whoever was using the meth was the real shooter. Although police had seized dozens of firearms from the Potter household, Fallin pointed out that the gun used to kill the victims was not among them and remained unaccounted for.

As the trial dragged on over five days, journalists, cameras, and curious onlookers filled the courtroom. They gasped at photos showing the bloodied young couple, Billie Jean's arms still outstretched as if holding the child that rescuers had already taken from his dead young mother. They heard friends of Bill and Billie testify to ongoing harassment by Jenelle, and later her family, after befriending (and subsequently unfriending) Jenelle on social media. They testified to how much the ongoing drama had affected and continued to affect their lives, and denied, under oath, making death threats to Jenelle, or writing the vicious messages Jenelle claimed they had sent her. They spoke of more than twenty calls a day that caller ID showed had come from the Potter residence. Deputies described Barbara ripping up evidence, including photos of Billie Jean and Lindsey attached to emails with degrading subject lines and captions. Although investigators had not found the gun in question, an expert testified that loose, unspent rounds found in Buddy's truck matched the rounds found at the scene.

The jury listened to recorded phone calls between Buddy and Barbara, including the one in which he seemed to confess and she quickly tried to provide him an alibi, and another in which Barbara said, "I got rid of it all. I got rid of the junk."

Christie Groover, the estranged daughter of Bud and

Barbara, testified to her troubled childhood, as well as the strained relationship she had with her immediate family, which she mostly attributed to her mother.

Witnesses testified to Buddy's constant claims of being affiliated with the CIA, including Sheriff Mike Reece, who recalled Buddy making the claim when he came in to complain about a county official unfriending his daughter on Facebook. Other witnesses testified to altercations between the Potters and the victims. JD Weinberger, who worked at the Food Lion, testified that Buddy had told him he'd like to put a bullet in Bill's head prior to the murders and had given him a "kill stare" when they talked about it in the days that followed. JD denied he was making up stories, just so he could be involved in the case for fun or publicity.

In response to claims that Buddy was denied oxygen during his interrogation, which led to him seeming to make a confession to his wife over the phone, a doctor testified that while Buddy's history of apoxia could have contributed to an impaired state of mind, there was no known cases of apoxia causing a patient to lie, and certainly not so profusely.

TBI Agent Scott Lott recounted details of his questioning of family and friends in the immediate aftermath of the murder about any enemies the young couple may have had. The only names that kept coming up again and again were the Potter family. It seemed nearly everyone in town knew about the bad blood between the victims and the Potters.

On Friday, October 11, 2013, after deliberating for just three hours, the jury announced they had reached a verdict. They found Marvin Enoch "Buddy" Potter Jr. guilty of two counts of murder in the first degree.

As the jury foreman read the verdict, Buddy showed no

emotion. He had remained stoic throughout the trial and appeared to be unaffected by the conviction, which under Tennessee law, automatically carried one life sentence per count. Bill and Billie Jean's families hugged and cried. Christie appeared to have mixed emotions about the fate of her father, who was the only member of her immediate family she still felt some affection for.

Despite the solid victory, ADA Brooks and his prosecution team felt it was incomplete, as Buddy Potter hadn't acted alone. In fact, in their opinion, he hadn't only been in cahoots with Jamie Curd. Brooks queried the jurors about what they thought of the days of testimony they had listened to and, crucially, how they felt about the culpability of Barbara and Jenelle Potter.

The feedback provided by the jury was that those two women were every bit as guilty as the man they had just sent to prison for the rest of his life.

20

JAMIE WAKES UP

Jenelle, Jamie, and Barbara were each set to face trial on two counts of first-degree murder and conspiracy to murder in a combined trial. Barbara also faced a charge of tampering with evidence, thanks to her ill-fated attempt to shred the emails and photos right under the nose of Chief Deputy Woodard.

Each time the trial date loomed, the court permitted further extensions, with the defense teams insisting they needed more time to sift through the electronic evidence and learn what the linguistics specialist hired by the prosecution might have to say about the content of the emails. The weeks stretched out and soon became months.

ADA Brooks believed wholeheartedly in his decision to proceed against the Potter women with the charge of first-degree murder, even though they had not been present when the murders took place. He agreed with the town's sentiment that they had manipulated the simple, lonely Jamie Curd to do something he would never normally do. Jamie had no prior history of violence and no criminal history to speak of. He believed that his girlfriend—the girl he wanted to marry and the only girl who had ever wanted anything to do with him—was being harassed and threatened, and that her brother was a CIA agent looking out for not only the Potters, but for Jamie as well. He was desperate to gain the approval of her family because Jenelle would not do anything without their support. All throughout Buddy's trial, and as his own trial approached, Jamie's loyalty to the Potter family was unwavering.

All that changed in early 2015, when the District Attorney received a call from Jamie's attorney to say that Jamie would cooperate with the state if that meant having a shot at freedom. The overwhelming mountain of digital evidence, carefully explained to him by his lawyer, had finally convinced him he had been both fooled by the woman he thought loved him, and exploited by her cruel, manipulative mother. But what was most persuasive was that the prosecution dug up evidence proving Jenelle had not been the faithful girlfriend he thought she had been. During their relationship, she had been declaring her love for a man by the name of "Bob Meehan," whom they had discovered was another online boyfriend of Jenelle's. Although they never met in real life, they corresponded regularly, and Bob sent Jenelle a ring she had demanded he buy from JC Penny for her. Bob ended the relationship when he discovered Jenelle had an actual boyfriend in the town where she lived.

Jamie Curd was once again back in court, this time arguing that they should sever his trial from that of the Potter women. Having read through much of the evidence, his attorney believed Jamie could come to an agreement with the prosecution to assist in their trial against his ex-girlfriend and her mother. Jamie's trial was rescheduled to begin at a date to be determined, following the trial of Barbara and Jenelle. Then the floodgates opened.

The prosecution finally had the story of what had really happened leading up to that dreadful night in January 2012. Jamie told of his love for the only woman who had ever seemed to love and need him, of his desperation to gain the approval of her parents, and his absolute belief that she had a friend called Chris, who thought of her as his little sister, and who would do anything to protect her. Why wouldn't he? Barbara had also acted as though Chris really existed, and there had been incidents that thoroughly convinced Jamie that Chris was real, such as Chris knowing things that Jamie had done during the day after following him, and Chris convincing Barbara that Jamie was a man to be trusted.

The way Chris wrote was in stark contrast to the way Jenelle communicated with him. Jenelle hated swearing, and her writing was always sweet and loving, with no threats of violence to others. Chris, on the other hand, would rant and frequently swear and wish pain and death upon the enemies of Jenelle.

Buddy also acted as though Chris existed and spoke as if the CIA was on standby to reactivate him at any minute. Buddy told Jamie that Barbara printed out the emails and showed them to him, as Buddy did not know how to use a computer. Jamie sincerely doubted Buddy even knew how to turn it on.

Jamie's own level of education didn't allow him to appreciate the significance of the many coincidences in the spelling, grammar, and punctuation of Chris's communications and those from Jenelle. Most other people who got involved in the Topix and Facebook feuds soon recognized the patterns and similarities in the posts by those who jumped in to defend Jenelle, and it was obvious they were all written by the same person. He also didn't notice inconsistencies in Jenelle's stories about Chris, or slip-ups she made when she confused things she had told him with those that were supposedly said by Chris.

It was only now, nearly two years after he helped to commit murder for the woman he loved, that Jamie was embarrassed and ashamed to admit he had been played. He wondered if Jenelle had ever loved him at all, or if she simply saw him as a way to get what she wanted, to get rid of her enemies.

The detectives needed to know: how exactly had the murders gone down. Jamie took a deep breath and began telling the most difficult part of his story.

21

THE NIGHT OF THE MURDERS

Jamie recounted that, on the evening of January 30, 2012, Barbara had called and invited him to the Potter residence to work on the computer. She had a bill that needed to be paid by midnight and claimed her computer was locking up so she couldn't pay it. She needed Jamie there urgently and Jamie was happy to drop everything and go to the Potters if it meant seeing Jenelle.

Buddy entered the computer room while Jamie was alone and asked if he would "do him a favor." Buddy asked Jamie to "take him down next to Bill's, let him out and go down the road and come back and pick him up." He didn't say when, but Jamie, always eager to win the approval of Jenelle's father, agreed.

Not long after Jamie got back home, Jenelle called him on his landline to tell him Buddy would need his help the next morning. Jamie told Jenelle that he wanted to work on his computer, and that he needed to hang up to use the phone line. The two then exchanged several text messages declaring their love for each other in the way teenagers do. At 2:21 a.m., Jenelle sent Jamie a text message saying she wished to "talk for just a little." They spoke for about 30 minutes, after which Jenelle wrote, "I love u. I would not take your cell phone with you in the morning love."

"I'm not goin' to," Jamie replied. The text messages finished with Janelle writing, "I love you my husband, and Jamie, you need anything you come here love."

In the early hours of January 31, 2012, long before the sun peeked over the horizon for the day, Jamie's home phone rang again, but fell silent before he could reach it. The caller ID showed that the phone call came from the Potter residence. He tried to call back, but there was no answer. It was 4:25 in the morning, but Jenelle was awake. She sent Jamie a text message instructing him to try again, telling him that if Buddy didn't answer, she would search the house for him.

This time Buddy answered and asked if Jamie could do that "favor" for him that morning. Jamie agreed, and moments later, Jenelle sent Jamie several messages in rapid succession, saying her father was leaving and telling Jamie to text as soon as he got back. She peppered the messages with declarations of love.

Under the cloak of darkness, and leaving his phone behind as Jenelle instructed, Jamie slid into the passenger door of Buddy's black Ford F-250 truck and settled into the leather seat. The two men drove to the parking lot of a church across a field from Paw Bill's house—a good vantage point where they could see people come and go. They waited until they saw the headlights of a pickup truck cut through the darkness, signifying that Paw Bill was leaving the house. Buddy motioned for Jamie to follow him and started on foot across the field. When they finished the trek, they hid behind a shed out back of the house. Jamie warned Buddy that if Bill saw them, "All hell's gonna break loose!"

Buddy handed Jamie a gun. Jamie looked down at the

weapon in his hand, a chill running down his spine. "I couldn't kill no-one," he told the older man. Buddy responded that he just needed Jamie to "stand at that door" as he held his own .38 caliber in front of him, prepared to do violence. Jamie had never seen Buddy like this before. It was as if his CIA training had suddenly kicked in and he was a man on a mission.

The back sliding glass door was rarely locked, and this time was no exception. Jamie stood guard as ordered, while Buddy strode down the hallway and entered the first bedroom. Jamie heard his cousin Bill utter the last words he would ever say.

"What the hell?"

Buddy would later claim that Bill pulled a knife on him and in the ensuing struggle, he "accidentally" shot the younger man. However, after that, he took Bill's knife and slit his throat deliberately "because of the things they were saying about my daughter."

Jamie watched from his lookout point as Billie Jean fled from the room after the gunshot rang out. Moments later, Buddy came out of the bedroom and looked at Jamie as though querying where his prey had gone. Jamie pointed down the hallway where Billie Jean had run, and Buddy took off in that direction. Jamie left his post to look inside the first bedroom and saw his cousin lying on the bed, blood pooling around him. When Jamie heard another gunshot, he ran from the house and back across the field to Buddy's truck.

Buddy was not far behind, and Jamie returned the gun to him, before Buddy dropped him off at the end of his driveway, where Jamie promptly threw up from shock. Desperate not to be alone, he went to visit his niece Lori at her trailer home. Lori was one person who he could confide in about his love for Jenelle, his distress at her being targeted by everyone in town, and her big brother in the CIA. She had been on the receiving end of many of Jamie's laments. That morning, Jamie told Lori that he had received a text message from "Chris" that said, "the problem was over."

A few hours later, Roy and Linda Stephens made their grisly discovery.

22

THE SECOND TRIAL

This is going to be the stupidest thing you've ever heard. This is going to be the craziest thing you've ever heard. There is nothing in your lives or backgrounds that has sufficiently prepared you to understand the Potter family. I can say, with complete confidence, that you have never seen anybody like them.

— OPENING STATEMENT BY ASSISTANT
DISTRICT ATTORNEY DENNIS BROOKS AT
THE TRIAL OF BARBARA AND JENELLE
POTTER, MAY 3, 2015

Upon the news of Jamie's defection, Jenelle and Barbara were once again given permission to push out the date of their trial. Avoidance was a technique Jenelle was accustomed to utilizing whenever something unpalatable was in her future.

Even with Jamie as their star witness, the prosecution was going to have a tough time making their case to the jury that Barbara and Jenelle, "acting with the intent to promote the commission of the offenses, solicited, directed, aided, or attempted to aid" Buddy and Jamie in the commission of the murders. The emails they had were a confused, jumbled mess, purporting to have come from different people, all wishing death upon the young couple, but it was difficult to point to a single "smoking gun" among them, where either Barbara or Jenelle had outright demanded that Buddy and Jamie go out and kill. The District Attorney's office was going to have their work cut out for them. Going through the electronic carnage methodically enough for a jury to both understand what was going on and be convinced that Jenelle was the author behind many false usernames was a herculean task.

Finally, on May 3, 2015, the Potter women went to trial. Each of the women had her own representation, though they would be tried jointly. In US courts, defendants are tried jointly when:

- Each defendant is charged based on the same or similar evidence
- Each defendant allegedly participated in the same acts or transactions
- The alleged crime involves a common scheme, conspiracy, or enterprise
- Proof of one charge requires proof of another

Gray-haired Barbara entered court each day in a wheelchair, although whether she truly needed it was up for debate. Jenelle dressed demurely, her big gangly frame making the clothes look even frumpier than they were. Neither of the women looked like your typical murderer. The prosecution was going to have an uphill battle convincing a jury that they should give these two frail and damaged women a life sentence for writing emails and social media posts.

Assistant District Attorney Dennis Brooks opened with his dramatic statement about the crazy ride the jury was in for as they heard about the Potter family. He then painted a picture for the jury of a lonely 30-year-old woman who had trouble making friends, destroyed the friendships she had, and created a slew of male personas to defend her online, including a "brother" who was in the CIA and would do anything to defend his little sister from those who wished her harm. He then told them about her bitter, interfering mother who loved the invention "Chris," but hated Jenelle's real-life boyfriend, Jamie Curd. He spoke to the jury for nearly two hours trying to do justice to the messy, ridiculous tale. It was ADA Brooks' longest opening statement ever. According to his book *Too Pretty to Live*, when someone admonished him and said he really should keep his opening short, "I told them that I had. That was as brief a summary as I could give."

Barbara's attorney, Randy Fallin, the same man who had represented Buddy, addressed the jury, describing his client as "a loving mother." He said that it was Jamie Curd who had the know-how and access to the computers, Jamie Curd who was behind the murders and the strange personas. Fallin said Jamie was upset because he'd lost his drinking buddy when Bill became involved with Billie Jean, and that he had laid the blame on Jenelle's parents because he wanted them out of the way so he could finally have Jenelle all to himself.

Finally, it was time for Jenelle's attorney, Cameron Hyder, to give his opening statement. He said the state's argument was all "smoke and mirrors," and told the jury, "The state will have you believe that Jenelle Potter coerced

Jamie Curd, a man eight to ten years her senior, to complete these acts." Some feat, he said, when "Jenelle Potter operated on the level of an eight or nine-year-old." The school system had put her IQ at 77, and a full psychological and neuropsychological evaluation conducted for the court case put it even lower, at 72, putting Jenelle about three levels below the average person. Hyder also cautioned the jury to remember that it's not illegal to "spew hate and vitriol over the internet," in an apparent admission that his client had done just that. The tactic of both attorneys was to paint Jamie as the Machiavellian orchestrator of the murders and their clients as simple, innocent bystanders.

On the second day, the jurors were taken through complex technical testimony. A TBI special agent in computer forensics testified to the legitimacy of the data and photographs extracted from the computer and cell phones. Tempers flared among the attorneys during cross-examination of the experts about what they should have been looking for and whether the existence of malware on the computer, which the defense would argue could have been placed there by Jamie, had been sufficiently looked for or missed. TBI Agent Scott Lott testified that the IP addresses he obtained from the internet service provider that were assigned to the Potter's computer matched those on the email headers from Barbara and Jenelle's accounts.

Another expert testified that emails and phone numbers could be "spoofed" so that the recipient thought they were receiving an email or call from one number, but it was really from someone else. The conclusion the jury could draw was that maybe those calls and messages had not come from the Potter household after all.

Agent Lott was grilled about not only the evidence he had collected, but also about evidence he did not. The defense attorneys demanded to know why he did not collect and bag cigarette butts from multiple ashtrays, or why the meth pipe found in the victims' bedroom was not tested for possible DNA evidence. Doing so may have placed someone else at the scene, given that autopsies on Bill and Billie Jean had not detected drugs in their systems.

The most unusual evidence was about the communications from "Chris." First, prosecutors had to convince the jury that Chris was not a real person, but an invention of Jenelle's. A linguistics expert took the jury through the similarities of the emails from Chris and words known to be authored by Jenelle. Over 209 pages, he noted that Jenelle often left a letter or two out of a word and capitalized words that did not require capitalization. She frequently used run-on sentences and transposed letters ("siad" instead of "said"). Jenelle's writing contained frequent separation of a single word into two words, such as "out side," and she often began sentences with "and." Jenelle failed to use double consonants where required before adding a suffix and left the "e" in the root word when adding "ing," for example, "leaveing" rather than "leaving." Chris made the exact same errors in "his" writing.

Once expert testimony was presented that the similarities between Jenelle's writing and the writing of "Chris" were so similar that the two were almost certainly the same person, ADA Brooks skillfully took the jury through the bizarre emails, in chronological order. As he did so, the story unfolded as to how the two women had manipulated Buddy and Jamie into doing their bidding.

The frankly ludicrous conversations between mother and daughter, without the mother knowing she was talking to her own daughter, were difficult for anyone to follow. But, when certain passages were highlighted, it eventually became clear that Jenelle had convinced Barbara that Chris from the CIA had nominated Jamie as a suitable person to assist Buddy in murdering Jenelle's enemies. Barbara passed on that information to Buddy, and the two of them convinced Jamie that he had the CIA's approval if he were to assist Buddy in slaughtering two people, including his own cousin. It was partly self-preservation on Jamie's part —after Jenelle lost her court case in November, Chris wrote to him to say that CIA surveillance intelligence discovered that Billie Jean had urged Bill to take revenge on Jamie because he had sided with the Potters. It was kill or be killed.

Jenelle, as Chris, also ramped up the pressure on her parents. Chris wrote to Barbara that Bill was spreading rumors that Buddy was dealing drugs, and that Bill, Billie Jean and Lindsey had devised fresh plans about how to kill Jenelle. Barbara provided Jamie with explicit information about the times Paw Bill and his son left the house to go to work, which was used to identify a brief window of time for the murders to be carried out.

It had taken almost a year, but Jenelle's incessant rants, emails, and messages had the intended effect of ensuring her mother, father, and boyfriend would all be willing to kill for her. And they did.

Jenelle's sister, Christie, was once again called as a witness. She was emotional on the stand as she spoke of the severed family ties which led to her moving out of the family home at the end of 1999. Christie told the court about her little sister, who had learning difficulties and a hearing disability and operated at the mental level of a young teen, but who had her parents "wrapped around her finger." She said she wanted to have a good relationship with Jenelle but said her sister made it difficult. "Jenelle had trouble understanding the difference between what's a joke and what's reality," Christie explained.

Christie also said that Jenelle was coddled as the favored child. "She knew how to play my parents." The defense tried to discredit her, but she was steadfast. She also denied that Jenelle was so intellectually backward that she was little more than a helpless child, saying she was an expert at manipulating her parents. "She is a slow learner," she said. "Her cognitive formulation is odd. But she is not as bad as you're making it sound."

While Christie may have felt residual love for her family, the jury was left with no doubt who was the favored child of her parents when they heard the shocking line in one email by Barbara urging Chris to kill her daughter, Christie, but ensure her body was found so that she and Buddy could collect the life insurance. There was nothing to indicate that Barbara was joking or fantasizing during this exchange. She genuinely seemed to want to see her daughter murdered.

A psychologist testified that Jenelle indeed had an IQ of 72, and that her hearing problems exacerbated her learning difficulties and ability to detect nuance in communications. He told the jury, "The allegation that she is in some way a mastermind or a manipulator or a planner, I think really flies in the face of the facts, which go back and say that she is functioning basically as a fourth grader."

"Can a nine-year-old be manipulative?" ADA Brooks asked the psychologist.

"Nine-year-olds manipulate their parents all the time," the psychologist conceded.

The prosecution also had a surprise witness. Christopher Tjaden appeared in court, tall and good-looking in his red and white plaid shirt, where he confirmed, to the surprise of nobody, that he had never been in the CIA, that he barely knew Jenelle, and that he had certainly not been in contact with her or any of her family since graduating high school. The real Chris seemed somewhat amused at the bizarre circumstances that had brought him to court. As Assistant District Attorney Matt Roark showed him photo after photo, message after message, Christopher responded each time with a smirk and said, "Nope. Not me." Jenelle's eyes never left him as he testified.

The prosecution also introduced 38-year-old Bob Meehan, another online boyfriend of Jenelle's. They really did have a relationship of sorts, but Bob and Jenelle's relationship had only existed on Facebook. They had never met in real life and Bob ended the relationship when he learned of Jamie. He recalled her also talking of her "brother" Chris who was in the CIA.

Johnson County Sheriff Mike Reece recounted his many encounters with the Potter family that stemmed from the social media and Topix feuds. He had found the constant complaints by the Potters to be petty and frustrating. He testified that he told Buddy Potter the best thing he could do was unplug the computer and throw it away.

Lindsey Thomas, Tara Osborne and Bill's sister, Tracy Greenwell, all took the stand and described years of harassment. Tracy also told the court that the real trouble from Jenelle started after Bill and Billie Jean's dating turned serious, and that it got worse after their baby was born. She also told the jury that Bill and Jamie had been close and never fought until Jamie began his relationship with Jenelle.

The star witness was Jamie Curd himself. He explained, in minute detail, what had happened on that fateful morning, from Barbara summoning him to the house the night before, to the messages from Jenelle telling him she loved him and warning him to leave his phone behind as she sent him off to slaughter her enemies. Jamie spoke of seeing his cousin with a bullet through his brain, and of blocking the exit of the young mother who desperately wanted to protect her baby. He said he never could have imagined he'd find himself inside his cousin's home, acting as lookout with a gun in his hand while another man gunned down the young parents.

Jamie testified he had believed that Chris was real, even long after the murders had occurred, and had only recently come to realize that Chris did not exist and had never existed. He knew now that the entire Potter family had manipulated him to do their bidding. "Well, I mean, I thought Chris was real. I mean, I thought that there was a ... you know, someone that I was talking to there, and Jenelle ... the way she would talk to me ... it was like a—a bonding ... a family. And it's like now it's all a lie."

"How does that make you feel now?" ADA Brooks asked.

"Ashamed. Humiliated. Stupid," Jamie said. However, while Jamie testified and blamed Marvin Potter for the murders and that he had corresponded with the mysterious Chris, he told the jury that the Potter women were not involved in the killing, and there was no conspiracy between them all.

For their part, the defense continued to shift all the blame onto Jamie. They said that with his access to the sole computer in Barbara and Jenelle's house, he could have made the posts and sent the emails from "Chris". It was, they contended Jamie who had instigated it all. The attorneys pointed out that Jamie had every opportunity to stop the murders—Buddy couldn't have carried them out without him—but he didn't.

ADA Brooks finished his closing statement by saying, "If you can't imagine these crimes happening without these women, then you know in your heart what your verdict must be. You have before you the two people most responsible for Bill Payne and Billie Jean Hayworth's untimely demise, and their baby that was left orphaned back in 2012. We ask you now to bring about justice for these deaths."

After the week-long trial, the jurors retired to deliberate. The prosecuting attorneys were left to wonder whether they had recounted the bizarre tale clearly enough to convince the jury that Barbara and Jenelle were as liable for the double homicide as the men who had been in the house that morning.

Eight long hours later, the courtroom was hushed as the jury foreman handed over the verdict to the judge, who passed it back so that it could be read out loud to the waiting press.

"Count one, we the jury find the defendant Barbara Mae Potter guilty of first-degree murder," the foreperson announced. And then, through each charge, for both women, the word "guilty" rang out seven times. The courtroom erupted.

Judge Blackwood sentenced both women to two life sentences, one for each count of first-degree murder. Barbara also received three years for tampering with evidence, to be served concurrently with her life sentences. Unlike Buddy, who had remained impassive upon hearing his sentence, Barbara and Jenelle both erupted into dramatic tears. Barbara, at sixty-four, would die in prison and Jenelle, at thirty-five, would likely be in her eighties before being eligible for parole.

The relatives of Bill and Billie Jean were even more emotional this time than they had been at Buddy's conviction. Everyone in town knew what a menace Jenelle was, and how much drama, hatred, and collective angst she had caused over the years. Few people had been confident that she would be made to pay for her crimes, let alone receive a murder conviction. Their relief was overwhelming.

Bill's mother told the press, "We're still hurting, we'll always be hurting. You know, Billy couldn't call me on Mother's Day." She also had a parting shot for Barbara Potter. Referencing one email that had been read out in court, she said, "Barbara, you wanted to know if you'd go to hell? Yeah, you're going to hell. And if I have to forgive any of you'ns to stay out of hell myself, I'll see you there."

Shortly after their trial, both Barbara and Jenelle, who were serving their sentences in the same prison, were interviewed on camera for the TV show *20/20*. Both continued to deny any involvement with the murders. Barbara flat-out denied that she was the author of any of the emails, still claiming to be the victim of Jamie who had used his cunning skills to make it look like she'd written them.

"I'm not that kind of person," she insisted. "I'm not evil." She said that she believed she would go to heaven, with a clean conscience.

Jenelle used a tactic that had always served her well. When the interviewer confronted her with the insurmountable evidence that she and Chris were one and the same person, she sobbed loudly and cried, "No, no, no!" until her lawyer insisted on ending the interview and ushered Jenelle away.

TBI Agent Scott Lott was also interviewed. He made every effort to try and distance the case from the narrative that it was all about social media, even though *20/20* had named the episode "Unfriended." Lott believed a much more common motive was at play. Jenelle Potter had an unrequited crush on Bill Payne and was furious that it hadn't been reciprocated. When Billie Jean came onto the scene, Jenelle was consumed by jealousy, which turned to hatred. He said, "It wasn't unfriending on Facebook. It was a jealousy issue. And someone with too much time on her hands."

If only Paw Bill had lived to see justice being done. But then, Paw Bill was such a gentle soul, perhaps it would have provided him with no pleasure at all.

23

PRISON AND APPEALS

Jenelle learned all her craziness from her momma. She's the key to the whole thing

— POST IN TOPIX THREAD "JENELLE POTTER STRIKES AGAIN"

On July 14, 2015, Jamie Curd, Jenelle Potter's former boyfriend, who had accepted a plea deal in exchange for his testimony and a guilty plea to the lesser charge of facilitation of first-degree murder, was sentenced to twenty-five years, with the possibility of applying for parole in less than eight years.

As he had already served over half of that, his first parole hearing occurred in November 2015, just a few months after his sentencing. ADA Brooks and the victims' families all opposed parole, with ADA Brooks saying, "It would be a slap in the face for the justice system if Jamie Curd were to be released so early in his sentence." The families organized a petition to keep him locked up, once again turning to social media to ensure it gathered as much support as possible. Parole was denied, with Jamie eligible to try again in 2019. There has been no news of him since, but he remains incarcerated in the Bledsoe County Correctional Complex.

In July 2021, Buddy Potter testified at one of Barbara's post-conviction hearings that it was Jamie who pulled the trigger on Billie-Jean. At Buddy's trial, Agent Lott had testified that the bullets recovered from the scene had come from two different manufacturers, but he could not say whether they had been fired from two different guns, or both had been fired from the same one, with one being a little undersized for that gun. The jury came to the conclusion that Buddy had killed both victims.

In his book, *Too Pretty to Live*, Assistant District Attorney Brooks expressed some sympathy for the awkward, lonely, uneducated man who had become the pawn of such a jealous, controlling, and vindictive girl and her overprotective parents. He wrote, "Had the Potters not come into Jamie's life, he would have gone to his grave without a single incident as a violent criminal. I truly believed that."

B uddy appealed his sentence, on the grounds that there had been insufficient evidence to find him guilty of both murders, and that a material witness for the defense, Jamie Stout, had failed to appear at court to testify, putting him in contempt of court. Stout was expected to testify that Brad Osborne had visited him at home on the day of the murders and told him that, contrary to what he had told the police, he had in fact found the bodies of Bill and Billie Jean that morning and had called his wife, Tara, from the house and asked her what to do. Tara allegedly told her husband to get out of there, because the police would put the blame on him, and Brad allegedly left the crying child with its dead parents. "He didn't go make a 911 call anonymously or otherwise, and so, it was our theory that he probably shot them," Buddy's attorney said.

Buddy was unsuccessful in his appeal. The court ruled that there had been sufficient evidence for the jury to find him guilty beyond reasonable doubt, and that had Mr. Stout testified as defense counsel anticipated, his testimony would have consisted of hearsay, which was inadmissible and would not have had any meaningful impact on Buddy's defense.

B arbara appealed her sentence on a number of grounds, including that there should have been a change of venue away from Johnson County due to the adverse publicity the case had received before trial, and that she believed her daughter's friendship with ADA Brooks was "inappropriate" and that he therefore should have withdrawn as lead counsel. The court denied these motions.

Barbara and Jenelle returned to court in 2017, demanding a new trial with a new prosecutor after ADA Brooks released a book, *Too Pretty to Live: The Catfishing Murders of East Tennessee*. The pair's defense attorneys claimed that there was vital information included in the book that was not disclosed to them during the normal discovery process. They argued that Brooks intentionally picked and chose what pieces of information from their meetings with Jamie Curd they would share at trial.

The defense included a letter in support of the Potter women, written by a corrections officer who had supervised them. The officer had taken a particular interest in Barbara and Jenelle and called their attorneys from her personal cell phone, telling them that both inmates' health issues were not being taken care of by prison staff, as well as passing on information regarding the delays in their appeals. To the judge, the officer wrote:

My name is [REDACTED], a Corrections Officer at Tennessee Prison for Women in Nashville TN. I've come to know Barbara and Jenelle Potter for the past year since they are inmates under my care. They are charged with a horrible crime which I believe they could not commit nor conspire to commit.

Barbara and Jenelle Potter never admit to intending to kill or neither hurt, nor conspiring to kill anyone because they know they are innocent. I have a lot of respect for Barbara and Jenelle Potter. They are neither deviant nor dishonest.

For me, Barbara and Jenelle Potter are honest people with good morals and character. They have lost everything they have except each other and there faith in God. In my humble opinion, neither Barbara nor Jenelle Potter could take that ill-fated step to further the act of taking the lives of two human beings.

Thank you and may God guide you in deciding the outcome of this upcoming hearing.

Such a measure was most unusual and inappropriate. The judge responded with a curt note to the corrections officer saying that he had to remain absolutely neutral. He told her not to send any more correspondence and later wrote a letter about the incident to the Department of Corrections. "It's not a crime, but you've got a state employee whose a corrections officer trying to influence the judge," the judge said. "I characterized it as poor judgement. In my opinion it was an attempt to influence the judge. No matter what happened, it needs to be investigated." The corrections officer was subsequently dismissed.

The retrial was denied. The court agreed with ADA Brooks that what was left out was irrelevant to the case. There remained overwhelming evidence of guilt, and therefore disclosing any of the extraneous information included in the book would not have altered the outcome.

Undeterred, Barbara and Jenelle continued to work at getting their convictions overturned, appearing in court several times more. Jenelle Potter's convictions were upheld, but in August 2021, Barbara Potter was granted a new trial after a judge ruled her trial attorney had a conflict of interest as he had previously represented Buddy Potter at his trial. In an about turn, however, Barbara rejected her chance at a new trial against the advice of her attorney. Instead, she pled guilty and reached a deal with prosecutors that sent her to prison for 25 years.

"It was not my advice to do that. It was my advice she proceed with a trial in this matter," Barbara's new attorney told the press. "But she wanted to conclude it and plead guilty to her part in what occurred. She didn't hesitate, not at all [when answering the judge's question about how she pleaded]. It took a lot of work to get here and I truly believe that she could have had a better outcome at trial. She certainly could have. But from Barbara's perspective, she'd already had that trial one time. She was thinking of that and of wanting to accept her fault in what actually occurred. She didn't have any hesitation. She truly wanted to accept her fault in what occurred."

At 69 years old, it is almost certain Barbara will still die in prison. But she will be with her daughter, the two of them housed in Tennessee Women's Prison.

24

ANTI-SOCIAL MEDIA

Wow, first and last time on these forums. I've came to the conclusion that some of you are really fucking nuts! Nuttier than squirrel turds. All you people have to do is spend countless hours on a forum arguing with each other? From what I gather, Jenelle is bat shit crazy, but it looks like some of you aren't too far behind her!

— POST IN TOPIX THREAD "JENELLE
POTTER STRIKES AGAIN"

Topix no longer exists in the same format as it once did, having long been supplanted by newer, shinier social media platforms, most notably Reddit and Facebook. Nevertheless, many of the vicious posts can still be retrieved from the online archive of the website. They show that Jenelle was not alone in posting vitriol and hate. Page after page depicted feuds, accusations and calls for violence or ostracization directed against numerous people. Far from being an outlier, the Mountain City forums were typical of small-town forums on the site.

In September 2011, when hatred was still festering and the feuds of Mountain City were gaining fresh momentum, *The New York Times* ran a feature about Topix, mentioning Mountain Grove in Missouri, another small town that fell victim to the "cesspool of character assassination" that was the Topix forums. The post topics and headlines were remarkably similar to those of Mountain City. That article also revealed that a woman in Indiana killed herself and her three children earlier that year after her divorce had been a topic of conversation on the Topix forums.

Six months later, *20/20* ran a story called "Innocent Man's Life Destroyed by Anonymous Topix Poster," which described the ordeal of a man dealing with the murder of his fiancée by her ex-husband. A Topix post discussing her death had deteriorated into vicious, untrue accusations against the man by anonymous contributors. As a result, he was shunned by his fiancée's family and lost his job. The perpetrator of most of the libelous posts turned out to be a woman he barely remembered, whom he had worked with ten years earlier, and who was hiding behind a variety of usernames.

Of course, Topix is not unique when it comes to platforms where online bullying is carried out, but the fact that it was largely unmoderated and allowed people to create and post from as many usernames as they liked was a major contributor to these incidents.

There is little doubt that Jenelle was not the only one taking advantage of the anonymity Topix provided to post toxic comments online. Many bored townsfolk joined in with gusto, some to further a personal vendetta, others because they enjoyed the spectacle. Bill admitted to Jamie that he had authored some of the posts attacking Jenelle.

There are many arguments for and against online

anonymity. Anonymous contributors on social media have been responsible for spreading disinformation, harassment and bullying, and hate speech inciting violence. It is unlikely people would partake in such ventures if they had to put their real names to their words. However, anonymity also provides safety for whistleblowers, and allows marginalized people to talk openly without fear of persecution.

Who knows what might have happened if Jenelle had not become immersed in her online fantasy world? Even if she had developed jealous feelings toward the partner of a man who didn't want her, she could never have orchestrated the destruction that followed without the anonymity social media provided her.

T*he following Appendix of contains a selection of unedited versions of key emails, social media posts and Topix discussions. The second story in this book comes after the appendices*

APPENDICES

SELECTED WRITINGS RETAINING ORIGINAL SPELLING AND GRAMMAR ERRORS

- Selected emails between Barbara and Jenelle Potter, Jamie Curd and "Chris from the CIA"
- Jenelle's police report
- Selected Topix posts

The second story in this book, A Bluegrass Tragedy, begins after these appendices

SELECTED EMAILS BETWEEN BARBARA AND JENELLE POTTER, JAMIE CURD AND "CHRIS FROM THE CIA"

The following are extracts of emails between Jenelle, Barbara, "Chris" (i.e Jenelle) and Jamie as reported by the court in transcripts of decisions in the court cases of Buddy, Barbara and Jenelle Potter. They have been reproduced verbatim and chronologically where possible. The errors in spelling, grammar and syntax have been left as they are in the originals.

In some cases, the court summarized the substance of the emails rather than repeating them in full. In others, the emails seemed to contain cut-and-pasted Facebook, Myspace and Topix posts. They are not a complete record, as many emails were destroyed, and some could not be reconstructed from the bags of shredded paper recovered from Buddy's pickup truck.

SEPTEMBER 30, 2010

Jenelle forwarded an email to Jamie that she said came from a friend, Brian G. Brian had forwarded Jenelle an email from an undisclosed alleged tormentor.

TO: JAMIE
FROM: JENELLE

[Alleged text of email from Jenelle's tormentor]

> OK did you see where Jenelle'slittle friend John is in
> jail and for touching and taking pictures of little girls
> and putting them on the net. EWWWW I hope he
> die's . I bet Jenelleis on it too. Eww she is so ugly
> anyways just look at her ugly face. and her Body eww
> she is sooo fat and she needs to lose a lot of weight.
> she ugly to look at . But anyways is with her ugly Ass
> and wont be with someone who would be kind to
> him and sweet and loving. He has even said How he
> hates her and dont like her and why is he even with
> her. he could do so much better, I hope she just kills
> her self. she is so mesed up. She is just little ass hole
> and she might be smart but she is ugly in every way.
> YUCK YUCK. she looks like a damn duck. I hope she
> gets killed soon. Billie Jean and Lindsey let this get
> back to her.

When forwarding the email, "Brian G" had written to
Jenelle:

> Jenelle, who in the Hell is doing this to you? Oh I'm
> madder then Hell and so is Shaun, You are not this
> person we all grown up together as great friends.
> God Jenelle You're a wounderful sweet careing kind
> hearted and kind and will do anything for anyone .
> And put everyone first before your self dear. I'm so
> soryy that you have ahd a rough life and you have
> always been a fighter and you stand up for others

and even try to see the best in everyone. I dont know these girls and I dont know why they are after you so much but you're a way better person Jenelle. You never saw it but it was up here too but the girls up here loved you and they miss you we all do but they are nuts down there. I told you I would never date a girl from TN this makes my point. dont pay any mind to them. What ever happends to John we will all pay for him. No one needs to die but if he did do it none of us can ever trust or be friends with him you know. Pray Jenelle your best at that. Love your friend Brian and tell Mom and Dad I said hello thank you.

Prosecutors tendered this email exchange with evidence from a linguistics expert that testified it was likely that both "Brian" and the tormentor were really Jenelle Potter.

JANUARY 1, 2011

FROM: CHRIS
TO: BARBARA

Hi Barbara

How are you? I hope you are well. Yes this is Chris AKA Cody. I'm so sorry to hear all of that is going on. I wish there was away tohelp you all. I cant come up there and see you if someone saw me it would not be a good thing. I hope to get out and talk tho. . . . I run by topixs b/c i saw that they said Jenelle was up here and with you both buddy and you and i saw it and got on there and i took care ofit they were doing nothing about it.

Chris told Barbara about his work with the CIA, claiming that he had "got rid of" people in Russia and New York. He wrote that he had shot "a lot of" people while working for the CIA. He explained to Barbara:

> I got toa point where they were bad ppl and i new it was us or them so i had to kill. But i love to shoot now. and Killing does not borther me at all.

Chris informed Barbara that, "at the office," he was known as "cody wize." Chris told Barbara that he could kill Barbara's daughter Christie Groover and her "family in PA." He said,

> i have each one of them inmy sights and i can get to them anytime. I just might.

Chris warned Barbara of potential threats to her safety and advised that she should not go to her mother's house alone. He wrote that he would work on getting "everything off" of Topix, noting that he had "so much on them all." He concluded with:

> I love you all
> your son Chris.

FROM: MOM BARBIE
TO: CHRIS

Barbara shared that Christie took her and Jenelle to court "in July/Aug to try to keep me away from my mother." She continued:

I warned my mom that she would come between us, and she has.

You and Buddy NEED to talk

I have trying to get him to come up to ask for Cody Wize and walk you outsdie so the girls out front can't listen and you can talk, then come to the truck and me and Jen will be in the back seat where no one can see us (black windows ya know) and we can say hello to you.

Buddy says if they kill me (heart/stroke,etc. /health pros. due to stress) that he will do what he was trained to do."

She told Chris that, if he wanted to meet with Buddy, to let her know when and where and that she would pass the message on to Buddy. She also encouraged Chris that:

as long as you are doing the right thing for mankind, then you will not be judged badly. If it is like Buddy did, you are helping others by getting rid of the bad.

Barbara also communicated her desire for Jenelle to have someone to:

take care of her and be good to her.

These guys down here are trash and we threw the last one out last year in Jan. - jerk Jamie Curd. He took advantage of me, & was dirty, muddy, and walked in the house any old time, even when Jen was in the hospital one time! He did not have good manners and smelled too. He used to hang out with Bill Payne, the 'maybe' father of Billie Jean Hayworth's baby, not sure yet, and he is running a whore house you know. We would not let her go out in the car with him bc he had a trap for a car and we did not have a trust with him. She did not want to go out with him either. She is such a good person.

She then transitioned to harassment by the victims:

We have no way to fight back. and when we went to the Sheriff's office, they gave us lip service. The guys' name was Brad Sutherland and he told us what a sharp computer kind he was and he'd take care of it all. Jenelle's 3 names disappeared once, but they added them back on. Isn't that awrful - Lindsey Thomas and Billie Jean Hayworth started it for some crazy reason bc they saw Jen out and got jealous of her looks . . . but we never joined topix and will never do so.

FROM: CHRIS
TO: BARBARA

As far as my Job Buddy can be called at anytime and might here in a few weeks We need all the CIA we can get to do a Job.

Buddy is 2ed on the list and I'm def on top b/c i'm in it. buti know a John is #1 and Buddy is #2 and then i guess iwill be called if they need me. I know Billie Jean hayworth and Lindsey and Bill . . . told them more then once to stop. and leave Jenelle and you all alone. But it didn't stop intill i had to say something. They are just mean girls lol.

FROM: BARBIE

TO: CHRIS

WoW!! I never knew how much I was hated or how much I am In Danger at all! Thank you so much for all of the information hon. I am going to print this and delete it, tell Buddy about it, and he will take action as needed and wait to hear from you if want to meet, etc. -ya know.

JANUARY 5, 2011

FROM: BARBARA
TO: CHRIS

Bill Payne has been in our home a few times, but not since Nov.2009. he brought that guy,Jamie Curd,up here to get Jenelle,& it made us mad bc he was not good for Jen at all. He told Jen to run away from home 5:30 a.m. in the morning last Feb.& he'd pick her up, but he didn't show . . . and Deputy Sean-Brown' picked her up, frozen, mixed up, a mess, and they called us to come up & get her. Then we had her call Jamie & tell him to not come around anymore, but it took some rough treatmt fr us to get rid of him; he wouldn't stop! Finally by end of March, told him off good, Bud warned him for the last time, &its over. The guys down here are basically no good . . . and she has finally found out. I don't know much about him, but he lives back in the holler, Jen would not survive long over there w/his old grouchy sick mom. She would have been alone most of time, tried to be a nurse for mom. But! She was so sorry she did that; he had her brainwashed & so scared& mixed up.

FROM: CHRIS
TO: BARBARA

Chris responded by defending Jamie, writing that Jamie "told everything" on Bill and that Jamie no longer went to Bill's house. Chris wrote that Bill had been "hateful" to Jamie since Bill began dating Billie Jean.

FROM: BARBARA
TO: CHRIS

Barbara stated that she did not know why "Jamie said good things about us" and said that "Jamie was not welcome here ever again." She referred to Buddy as "a sharp shooter & sniper" and indicated that Buddy was "ready." She also wrote:

Bud says to tell you that he has a Son that has kept him pretty informed thanks to you.

JANUARY ??, 2011

FROM: CHRIS
TO: BARBARA

I know Billie hayworth and Linzsay and Bill and Bill has told a few of us thathe told them more then once to stop. and leave Jenelle and you all alone. But it didn't stop intill i had to say something. They are just mean girls lol. Chrsitie is also friends with Linzsay and that's someone that awful to even know. Her brother is injail for stelling and also doing drugs and selling big time drugs and aslo Meth soshe has no room to talk about anyone. She has done the same thing. She just crazy. But Chrsitie is who you need to look out for. she is after you all a lot. and after what i saw in the court room she wants you dead and out of the pictrue. I'm so mad Barbie i dont know what to do. But if anything happends to you. She is gone for good or maybe before.

FROM: CHRIS
TO: BARBARA

I'm so sorry about your house and your truck and your car and Chrsitie doing nasty thing behind your backs. Yes she has asked guys for Sex and blow jobs for money. and they have not. they say either they are married or they dont want too. Also your Mom is no Angel. She is going behind your backand talk- ing about you to friends and also family. I have to get back to work . They are calling me from the spot i'm in.

MARCH 2, 2011

FROM: BARBARA
TO: CHRIS

They are watching our house all the time, threw stuff on the roof, yard, etc. grrr.) I'm not strong enough to fight back yet . . . but I will be at some point. Bud is angry!!!!

MARCH 3, 2011

FROM: BARBARA

TO: CHRIS

Bud was wondering When he would be contacted to meet and pick up his ID you spoke of some time ago. Just for YOUR info, He IS home every day now (as I am home), he can come alone bc Jen can be w/me,. HE is Actually wondering IF there is an ID or not!

FROM: CHRIS
TO: BARBARA

Yes I saw the ID they have not gave it to him yet??? That's what makes me so mad they say they will do it and they have not called him. I even TOLD my BOSS about it and he said yes and that he would get Tommy to talk to him. I don't understand them I will say something for Buddy b/c he does have it and I have seen it and is just like ours.

FROM: BARBARA
TO: CHRIS

Thanks for bugging them anyway Chris, but if they have decided Not to give the ID to Bud, we have to understand. He'd really like to be involved in a lot of things, espec. Christie, cuffing her when time comes, etc.

FROM: BARBARA
TO: CHRIS

Jen ran into Lindsey yest. At RiteAid & Lindsey said, "Your day is coming." To Jen. Jen stood up to her and said "Why wait?" "I dare you to touch me here and now." And Lindsey backed off some & acted tough, but she's not w/o All her rotten no good so-called friends . . . ha! I was proud of Jenelle &as far we say, Jen will Never be alone w/o one of us in the trucks or with her in a store, so THEY better Watch Out! We are Tired of all of this shit Chris! 7 yrs. Is 7 yrs. Too many & it is soon going to have to be over. (You are welcome to shoot any of them, but let Christie's body be found-we have life ins on her so may as well collect it...I know that sounds mean for a mom to say,but she hates me, wants me dead as well as Bud & Jen..)

Thanks for fighting for Bud & the ID-it's time for the talk to be over-he is ready for action (you know what I mean).. he can leave me now and do whatever they want

APRIL 5, 2011

FROM: CHRIS
TO: BARBIE

[about protection order taken out by Tara against Jenelle]

They better not ever put either of you in jail.

Chris wrote that he had a new boss but that he would try to get someone to call Buddy, explaining that Buddy was:

in the computer they can look him up and he comes up CIA so he can be called for anything.

FROM: BARBIE
TO: CHRIS

George,atty, told us loudly after judge was done, court done, "you have to talk to the magistrate & mayor and let them know what is happening to you, your property, harassment. he needs to know." ...And Mike told them all plainly in front of Bud last Tues.4/5 that they were to leave us all alone & to turn Tara away, no more false reports unless she has proof - so that is what she is doing now - making up emails galore(had some w/her lasst week in court,but no one wanted to see them).She complained bc some man is calling her but Jen doesn't know who that man/men are. She's stupid for a nurse! Jen is only on her own facebook but her friends have told her that they have seen the fake one & fb does not allow one to have more than one fb at a time... and Jen's had this one for at least 5 yrs. when it came out...they need to back off.

Bud is sooooo mad &I'm 100% behind whatever happens. You guys meet when you are ready Chris. Maybe Bud will have ID by then & can use CIA guns, etc. for his protection - get the jobs done. ya know. They all need to go& the ones left need to be given a big scare as they watch & wonder "am I next?"....

Whatever/whenever you want to do whatever, contact Bud. Did you tell your bosses/guys work w/you? Prob. not do that bc he h as no ID.ya know. Bud knows this area well & will help you he said. He is fed up & ready. Shame they had to push him to this bc he is a very patient man, but once you push him to hard too long, its over. He won't take it. Good you hve a list, but don't let anyone see it. I'm sure you have it memorized. Keep scaring up these 3 girls w/guns,etc. &breaking their cars, Chr's too. Make things hard for them bc they are making life hard for us.

Thanks Chris. Son, you take care. I am praying for you & for us. Its getting scarier now. Oh my goodness. Keep telling the cops to stay away from our house/road checking on Jen&Bud &Why???are they? grr Bud is mad about it bc has seen them; Mike needs to know this.Bud&Jen do nothing wrong,illegal nothing. They are good like me. Now I'm going to be getting our some; have driven against yest.& did fine other than worry about cop harassment. I drive Bud's truck usually now. (I agree w/ your statements bout getting them all....all th way - they aren't going right by m.cty.,let alone us)

Well Chris, I hope that you are starting to feel some better. I can't imagine how badly you are bruised up inside & out plus a broken arm, hurt back and neck . grrr &Mike is the reason. Well, he can be taken care of too by you all- huh? That was mean & dirty-not good at all bc he wants You dead! proved that much. Take care. Hope to hear from you soon. I/We love you son... and praying for your healing & rest, asking God to hear your prayers also. I'm glad you & we are Christians, something no one can take away from us...! Byeee for now! :) hang in there. Love you. Mom.

APRIL 6, 2011

FROM: BARBARA

TO: CHRIS

He let her know that Lindsey was down here, bragging at how she, Tara, Billie were going to 'get Jenelle' & are planning to come back 2nite- going all over town rounding up help to return tonight w/Tara & Billie to finish the job on the truck, Jenelle, whatever... Buddy is in "Vietnam Jungle Recon Mode" & they don't want to mess w/that... before he got back home, Chris Campbell took Jenelle off his facebook! Some friend huh?

APRIL 16, 2011

FROM: CHRIS
TO: BARBARA

Chris wrote that "Mike" [Sheriff Mike Reece] was bad news and that he could not wait to kill Mike. He then said:

Next is Lindsey andBillie Jean and Bill and then cops i want to get.

He also referenced the CIA ID and informed Barbara that Buddy was

in the computer as CIA and that's all that matters.

Chris expressed concern about Jenelle's well-being because

those girls have really broke her

and he reiterated that he would

kill them

Barbara wrote about carrying a weapon and Chris encouraged Barbara to do so and told her that Bill and Billie Jean were "talking really bad about Jenelle." Chris reiterated that he would kill Lindsey "and Bill then Billie Jean for sure. Then cops." He then wrote:

FROM: CHRIS
TO: BARBARA

> Well buddy can kill them before they will so no worries there. Dumb bitch ho. She needs her butt kicked good and left. And maybe run over and a bullet in her head. Then she would be a dead pan whore face bitch. LOL Karma it will come back on her. I hate everyone one of them. LOL.

APRIL 21, 2011

FROM: JENELLE
TO: BARBARA
RE: WHAT LINDSEY SAID

The email appears to contain a copy of an antagonistic email allegedly sent from Lindsey Thomas to Jenelle. In the message the writer identified herself as "Lindsey," called Jenelle names, and threatened Jenelle, writing:

> you're ass is mine your a fucking bitch remember that I can get you and will. your daddy cant do shit to me. I'm above the law dumb fucking bitch.

APRIL 27, 2011

FROM: BARBARA
TO: CHRIS
RE: HAPPY BIRTHDAY

> Happy birthday! It is amazing that you & Jenelle were born on the same day, same year, 1 minute apart & at the same hospital! you're the same age too. Isn't that quite a coincidence?

MAY 10, 2011

FROM: CHRIS
TO: MOM BARBIE

> I wish I new someone that would kill her while I'm here. But if you want a kill her and nothing will be asked for sure. I mean a missing person is a missing person.

Later in the message, Chris told Barbara that he feared that if Jenelle went to jail, she might commit suicide. He then offered that everything would "be alright," concluding

> I'm sure Buddy is on top of everything.

MAY 12, 2011

FROM: BARBARA
TO: CHRIS

Barbara updated additional acts of harassment that now

included acts toward Jamie. She expressed fear that the Potters' and Jamie's homes would be set on fire.

JUNE 1, 2011

FROM: BARBARA
TO: CHRIS

If you come back, do you have 'plans'? like talked about before for her espec. And for others? I hope they will let you do what needs to be done, and Bud is ready to help you. Though he needs an ID, he says in this town, they only look at the computer. He has thought and thought of ways & is ready...just needs another guy.

JUNE 13, 2011

FROM: MOM
TO: JENELLE

Remember I'm here if you want to talk. Dad don't mean to sound like he don't care. He is trying to make you think it is nothing, but all things bother him, they do . . . he talks to me about it. He is concerned, but doesn't want to worry you. I care; you know that. I do all that I can and

I'm here to listen and plan or whatever you need....just come to me. K? K.

JUNE 21, 2011

FROM: BARBARA

TO: CHRIS

anyway, a note to let you know this....I called Jamie this evening & talked for a while, then Bud talked to him. He is coming here on Thurs at noon to see us/talk for a while...so will try to tell you some in 'code' but he can tell you All –if he wants to.

[questioning why Chris had never called or met with her and Buddy]:

I can't imagine why you are so-o-o afraid of your bosses & 'other' ppl here bc thats just not right It just isn't. U'reBosses are not professional at all & are conducting themselves badly, so they, along with you all, could 'lose face' here in this town
    I dread the future w/Billie Jean , so hope she won't go after Jen (& us) next - w/the baby due soon, she should be concentrating on that, but she's not! Amazing to me!

JUNE 30, 2011

FROM: CHRIS
TO: BARBARA

I know Jamie said he was so sorry about all of that stuff. but he said you were always good to him and his mom. and he said nothing bad about any of you all at all. He's just mad about how they are buging You all and Him and he wont take it. He would kill her if he had someone he siad. He know's some ppl that would help him but he said trusting someone you know. He don't want anyone to talk. But yes i think if he and buddy would meet it would be a good thing. Before July 27th and let him tell you how he found out everything and he know's them girls was well so he can pretty much tell you if your going to have any isssues with Bill or Billie Jean next and he know's a lot. . . But please just talk to him .

I'm not sure what Lindsey and her boyfriend are up too and her Dad is not a man to mess with. But i still think buddy can take him down if he had to come to that. Now i know why ppl take care of there own issues with ppl kill themand no one cares. pretty much. I have head it and seen it for my self. I got ride of 2 and no one cared nor asked anything. lol. you can get away with it. She needs to be killed and Billie Jean and i don't care if i killed that baby and her b/c she going to make it into her. Who wants that shit fucking asshole's and whores. makesme so sick.

FROM: BARBARA
TO: CHRIS

Bud will call Jamie

JULY 2, 2011

FROM: BARBARA
TO: CHRIS

About Jamie, yes, everything's okay with us about way back then.We don't dislike him in any way. Bud really wants to meet with him but he thinks he works all the time. I told him to give him a call and meet him out somewhere or over his house. It needs to be done asap.He says he will He has been worried about me bc I've been so bad w/pain, but I told him not to worry bc sooner or later, things will get better at least I'm praying for that. So he will meet with Jamie, I'm sure, before 7/27!--hopefully he will be able to talk to our lawyer &possibly go to court w/us to speak if lawyer says so. We'll pay him. Bud wants to meet w/him . . . he just kind of thinks that Jamie can't help him w/anything,ya know, like he'd like,so he don't know if info would do him any good. He is upset that if Jen goes to jail-ya know & then when Billie starts on Jen after court in addition to Lindsey again . . . we just need to get away from it.

...

No, I don't think anyone would really mess w/Buddy. No one has seen the 'other side' of him - not in this town. He always comes across as a gentleman, but he know lots of stuff-ya know to do and say to get things rolling right. He's trained to rock n' roll..ya know. The time will come he thinks&he has thought it out. I'd love to say more, but better not here . . . the reason he wants to meet w/you.

. . . .

I'm glad that Jamie is really mad & if he feels like Bud, they may take care of some things pretty good. We all need peace in this place till we move away. I hope they meet soon...we don't know if he's around this next weeks or not or working every day, so have to call.

OCTOBER 9, 2011

FROM: JENELLE
TO: JAMIE
RE: this is from linsdy from c.

Your a fucking Bitch and you know your fucking ass
is going to jail and Bill is going to kill you he has said
that and i hope he does. None of us want you around
nor living. Your a wasit of air and time on everyone.
You are nothing. You really think you are sweet and
smart HAHA yeah right your dumb and your very
ugly no one wants you. Billie Jean thinks your fat and
Bill Me Fucking linsday i just hate you're a live. you
will die bitch and i cant wait to see it. go to Hell bitch.

OCTOBER 25, 2011

An email exchange between Chris and Jamie concerned
Jamie's going to see Jenelle, who was "sad." Jamie wrote that
Jenelle "need a break from here" and that he wanted "to
make her happy an give her pce of mind."

FROM: JAMIE
TO: CHRIS

no they shouldn't an def not her is to good of a girl to
have to put up with this shit an man words can't start
to say how much i love her i see the love she has for
me an thats something i thought id never see not
from this shit hole but she is my ray of light at the
end of the tunnel

FROM: CHRIS
TO: JAMIE

Jenelle really loves you man she has never loved anyone like she loves you i see it all over her. and you are very blessed for sure. and you have a great girl and these's mother fuckers just want tomake her life hell and i hope she dont think about killing her self. she has you to live for. and her Mom an Dad.

FROM: JAMIE
TO: CHRIS

i think that if it wasnt for us she might have thought about it didnt say it but i can tell she is just took all she can take an thoes motherfukers wont let up there crazyer than hell idk why they have to do this i know there life has to sux to the point that they see this as a sick joy or something dumb bastards

FROM: CHRIS
TO: JAMIE

i agree withyou man and it's sad they have to do this to Jen and herfamily and you and it's not right you know. It's so sad. I'm sad and i do pray for you all. And she just put upsome new pics on facebook you might want to look she is cute.

FROM: JAMIE
TO: CHRIS

just to see Jen happy makes my day i am blessed she is a gift from GOD she showed me what love is an thats something i thought id never find id gave up till i meet her i love to see her smile

FROM: CHRIS
TO: JAMIE

Hi Jamie

It's Chris, I wanted to say hello and I thank you for being there for Jenelle and Her Mom and Dad. They are good people and what others say about them is wrong. I know you have taken up for Her family and her. It means a lot to me. Well Anyways I hope you all can get her out on saterday and also you can still do what you wanted. Make sure you have Candles and make sure you have a card and make the bed really pretty and just love on her. Thank you for being the one there for her. She need's you in more way's then one. she is a wounderful sweet careing girl. She would do anything for anyone before her self. But i know you know this about her.

She is a good person. These's girls are just driving her so crazy and you know they are crazy. But what they are doing is still fucking wrong and hurting her like they are. There is no reson for it. Just b/c she is sweet and very pretty prettyer then them. They need to get over it. They just love to pick but from what i know. This Demon thing came to us from them. I think it really came from Lindsey and Bill from what I'm hearing and learning from. It's waiting on him and something will happen to them in time. With you and Buddy I hope you all can get them. I hope it all works out great. I hope that you will pray about it and Buddy is and that you know what you are all doing is great. Your going to help the town.) wish i could kill them but right now i really can't. But anyways I'm so happy that you and Jenelle are happy together and love each other so much. Have Lori call Jen and ask her to go out on saterday. thank you. But pray for Jenelle i know she is having a very hard time and she just needs someone like you and I'm so happy and blessed she has you.

Well take care dude and I love ya. You are my brother and thank you for being a true blessing to my Sister. Take care and God Bless

Chris

FROM: JAMIE
TO: CHRIS

I just wnt to make her happy an it hurts i cant do it more ofen she is my everything her happiness is my sunshine.

OCTOBER 30, 2011

Several more emails were exchanged, with Chris detailing the harassment and its effect on Jenelle i.e., "it's going to kill her," and how much Jenelle loved Jamie.

Jamie then responded, expressing his devotion to Jenelle and his frustration with the circumstances. He also shared that he was intimidated by Barbara and Buddy and wrote that it was like "walking on egg shells." Chris assured Jamie not to "worry about" Barbara, that Barbara would "be fine."

Chris coached Jamie on how to find favor with Barbara by showing Barbara how much he cared about Jenelle and calling and talking with Barbara.

FROM: CHRIS
TO: JAMIE

Jenelle is just at her end and from what Barbie say's all of this is getting to her so bad and she is worryed about Jenelle. But i think more you hang out and everything with them and then you and Jenelle alone it will all be ok you know. Man i have our back always and Jenelle never been happy or loved like you give her and she loves you and want's you and need's you and will always be happy and loved by you.

NOVEMBER 1, 2011

Barbara sent Jamie an email about the "junk" on Topix. She stated that she was "highly pissed" about the "hurtful, lies." She wrote that the Topix postings had "upset" Jenelle and were making Barbara sick. She wrote:

but good ol Chris went after them big time as 'Matt Potter' and he tells them off something awful.

FROM: BARBARA
TO: JAMIE

I feel bad for you bc how they run you down, its terrible. You are not the bad person they li ke to say you are....they even told the police last year that you were in trouble & bad & to keep you away from our house! . so you see? Can't trust Bill or any of them. I feel bad for you. Know this. You are Not alone. We are here and we care bout you a lot.

I know they think that I'm a little sweet lady who won't do anything but just smile and be nice to them, never carry a gun, but they are dead wrong....I hide my anger and readiness well.

NOVEMBER 7, 2011

FROM: BARBARA
TO: JAMIE
RE: HI JAMIE – ITS BARB – ONE MORE FAVOR FOR ME/BUDDY?

Barbara asked Jamie for more help with their computer. Specifically, she asked Jamie to remove all of Jenelle's postings on Topix as well as a specific "statement about Buddy," questioning whether Buddy had received a medal during his military career. Barbara told Jamie that Jenelle "had a bad evening," attributing a recent incident of harassment as the cause.

NOVEMBER 10, 2011

FROM: CHRIS
TO: JAMIE

Chris expressed anger about more acts of harassment toward the Potter family. He wrote:

I can't wait for you and Buddy and us to do our Job's.

He assured Jamie that he should not be concerned about Barbara, but encouraged Jamie to call and"talk to them."

"Chris" routinely concluded his emails with "Love always your brother,""your brother," or "Love your Bro."

NOVEMBER 16, 2011

FROM: BARBARA
TO: JAMIE
RE: Hey Jamie –Weds..... 11/16/11 ---- READ ASAP.

Hi Jamie -

Thanks for all of your help and support thru this thing. We're all tired but up. I'm getting a shower and laying back down - unless end up getting Jen something or to the ER/or hospital w/her.

I just wanted to tell you that I looked at Your Facebook account to see if Lindsey said anything to you at all and your comment to her is Gone! You might want to go into it again -- jackwright94yahoo.com is your email and your password is "mexall"

Just go into Facebook(thru typing it on search line on google or yahoo), then type in your email and password (see above), enter, & you're into your own FB-facebook page--Jack Wright's. :) Then on the search line at top of Your FB page just type in Lindsey Thomas and she comes up. I looked at her page, but don't see any mail from you to her may have to try again....

....

I did write to Chris earlier and tell him to never use last names on facebook but the ones he wrote in the other night he has already deleted anyway (but they'll show up in cookies; right? right) ..but Bill has a copy/pic of that screen now anyway so he will go after Jen for that & lots of other things that are in his little brain I'm sure. They are all 'fixated' on Jenelle, and/or us! grrr But anyway, its Chris that is putting their whole names on, not Jenelle. He added another topic on Topix called, Lindsey Thomas, Lindsey Potter and Billie Jean Hayworth - and is telling them off again--you can see it.... I know Bill thinks that this is all Jenelle, or us, doing this - but its Not and I explained it all to Chris anyway.

Jenelle is very sick, throwing up and shaking today, so it doesn't look good. She may end up at the hospital again, but Buddy will Still be around for later on.

NOVEMBER 23, 2011

FROM: BARBIE
TO: JAMIE
RE: Hi Jamie – from Barbie --------About our phone call today 11/23/11.

Barbara relayed Chris's warning to Barbara about Bill Payne's and Lindsey Thomas's plan to "get Jenelle in jail" before "going after" Buddy and Barbara. Chris said that Bill was "doing a lot behind J.s back."

He said:

Let J know this bc he is after him big time . Bill's always back stabbing and he's been doing this to J for more then just 2 years. J has no idea.

At the close of her email, Barbara told Jamie that he should call and speak to her or Buddy "about 'things' anytime" and stated that Buddy was "'stuck' about what to do now"

But it sounds like Bill has been after you for years before you knew us at all! They are trying to kill Jenelle little by little (but doc says that at this rate, it could happen anytime w/heart attack/stroke, DKA itself-that she is getting it too often now & the stress has to stop)...They won't stop until we're all dead/gone and the cops are behind Bill and Billie Jean and Lindsey Thomas per Chris.

By the way, If you talk/text with Chris,ask him if he thinks the cia will back up Buddy if he takes it into his own hands.

DECEMBER 6, 2011

FROM: BARBARA
TO: CHRIS
RE: SEND LATER – WHEN WILL GO THRU –TUES, 12/6/11.

So Bill and Billie Jean may as well accept the loss and go on w/their lives be they are Not going to get Jenelle. there is no way. Between our heavy quantities of ammo and protection of her at all times and your all's they are going to get the surprise of their lives. And as far as J goes, he's safe and he knows it. He don't want to be messed with and he is heavily armed and ready thanks to dad. lol so let them try to get to him.

...if someone wants to bring it on, they will All die, including the baby...

[Bill, Billie Jean and their friends] better think twice if they want to live any longer.

Barbara wrote disparagingly about Bill and Billie Jean and mentioned the incident that occurred after court at the convenience store, explaining that Buddy "was going to fight and kill Bill, had it in his mind plan-ready to go" but that Bill had "backed down"

Barbara then asked Chris,

So you think that it will be in a week or so - things will be happening - we are thinking different/sooner..and ready . . . well we will see - it may be sooner than anyone thinks...we want peace and no one here wants to kill anyone, but we will...."Bud is trying to be patient for the 'right time' but now, he says the Time is Has Come-whenever now! -and If they want Jen so bad they can't stand it, then come on! and they will breathe their last breath..bud is soooo ready, we all are.

She wrote about the local law enforcement being "useless," that she carried two guns, and that she would do whatever she had to do "to save my kid or myself."

She stated that she did not call 911 anymore because

we are ready to take care of this ourselves, espec. Bud and Jamie are super ready all the time...you said that their backs are covered well and that all is good--but dad knows that but says that he will do whatever it takes no matter whose around, but all is okay anyway& thanks . . .we never know if you hear all, see all or not, but we're all ready. They are glad cia is around but they say that they will be able to handle it all but good to know.

...I'll do whatever it takes to save my young!

...I will kill if I have to, not just hurt but kill

DECEMBER 12, 2011

FROM: BARBARA
RE: PRINT –Messages fr/to Chris-week of December 4, 2011-them harassing, etc.

But round 3 is Bill wants to hurt Jenelle or just yell at her he has not made his mind up yet. from the phone call's there are a lot of guys looking for Jenelle and know's her now. and She will be fine like I said she never alone. They are wanting to hurt her for many reasons. But it will be ok. as you know what I mean.

Please tell J and B it's ok and we have there backs and to just make you and Jenelle safe

FROM: BARB
TO: CHRIS

Anyone who wants to mess with Jenelle or w/us is Asking to die!

She then referred to the victims and their friends as

a bunch of druggies, dumb asses, evil satan worhsippers who have no brains for anything but harassing ppl & evil plots. They are not even ppl - they are monsters w/names.

DECEMBER 14, 2011

FROM: JAMIE
TO: BARBARA

> Jamie offered to
>
> get rid of the files that slow yr computer.
> ...I hope every oneis doing good an Bill an Billie
> Jean an Lindsey will get whats coming to them.

FROM: BARB
TO: CHRIS

> What are your feelings if someone was found w/a
> hole in them somewhere in a car? have you done
> this? Would they chk it out or not?

FROM: CHRIS
Posted to Jenelle's Facebook

> TO BILL PAYNE, BILLIE JEAN HAYWORTH,
> LINDEY THOMAS AND TARA AND BRAD AND
> ECT: PLEASE LEVE JENELLE ALONE AND STOP
> WITH THE HARASSMENT AND STOP TRYING
> TO RUN HER LIFE. LOOK AT YOUR OWN LIVES
> AND WORK ON THAT. B/C YOU ALL ARE JUST A
> BUNCH OF WHITE TRASH NO GOOD UGLY
> PEOPLE THAT LOVE TO HURT OTHERS WELL
> YOU NEED TO THINK OF THIS TAKE CARE OF
> YOUR KIDS BILL AND BILLIE JEAN AND LINDEY
> GET OFF YOUR METH DRUGS AND STOP
> GOING AFTER MY SISTER AND MY FAMILY

THANK YOU. ORYOU CANJUST GO JUMP OFF A
MTN FOR ALL I CARE YOU ALL NEED TO GET
OUT OF MY SISTERS LIFE.

JANUARY 16, 2012

FROM: BARBARA
TO: BARBARA

Can God Forgive a Murderer?, Christian News (LINK)
   billy graham-questions about forgiveness & murder -
AOL Search Results (LINK)

POLICE REPORT BY JENELLE POTTER

In May 2013, Jenelle wrote a report about an alleged incident for the police. Prosecutors later used this supervised example of Jenelle's writing to compare with emails and posts written by her various pseudonyms

Doing the month of May My Mom and I were in Mtn City Phar.We were meeting with the Pharmacist and picking up my new Prescriptions re my Brittle Diabetes. and i was standing at my mom's right sholder trying to listen to the Pharmacist and Janie Henry came in and saw me and give me looks then she walked in back of me and said she was going to meet me outside and "kick my ass" and then i got really upset. At that point a guy starting talking to me about my upset at that point my mom walked to the front door and Jaine was siting in the car waiting for me and then this guy went out and looked as well and said she was still there . At this point Mom Barbara called 911 to help us get out safely. Well the town cops had-ken Lane-Joey Norris come and i had went out to the car with him and he was geting my info and then this girl in a blue shirt came out of the Pharmacy and she was pissed because she siad that janie has to use the bathroom and janie said that she was scared of me and that she didnt do anything to me. And i told her it was none of her business and to go away . But then she new Ken Lane and i walked back in to the Phar. and sat down and then Joey Norris was looking at the tape still and i was waiting but then we got all my meds and left but Ken Lane was still out said waiting to see if we were safe and i told him thank you. Then Mom and I got in the car and went home from there.

After the Phary. I have gotten threats sence this has happened from Janie Hanery, Tracy Greenwell, Tara and Brad Osborne,-__? Allen he is in his 50's and said he was going to rape me and he would like to see me dead. Steven Dugger, Nicky Church Yelton, Lindsey Thomas, Jason Greenwell and Clay Greenwell, Tim Anson Christie Kay Groover Potter, my so called older sister. And Husbands and boyfriends and also friends i dont know names. They all have said i killed Pal Bill but he had cancer and other things wrong. And Tracy also has said he wants to kick my Ass and they have broken in to my phone and left me text meg. Tracy and Janie Henry have been up my road and then Tracy has been there. More then once. Yesterday i got her on tape going up my road she was up to something and then when i was over in Va the other day to see my Doctor at the Hosptial they left stuff in my lane. and Yesterday a 2 guys in a black Ford truck threw a bullet and caseing in my lane at me while i was geting stuff out of my dad's truck in to my Mom's car and they called me a Fuc**** Bitch. and they went so fast down the road. My Mom was staning on our front Porch and saw this. Then about 12 Am Tracy was parked in the down belong lane in out mexcains lane. Jessica Teaster came in to Randy Fallin's office and said she didnt want me there and i was a bitch and hope i get Killed.

SELECTED TOPIX POSTS

Various Topix posts presented in court, determined to have been authored by Jenelle Potter during her feud with Bill Payne, Billie Jean Hayworth and Lindsey Potter

Dan White AOL, United States Apr 21, 2010

Wow Matt and Kelly. I new she was bad but I had no clue she was off on the deepend. She is crazy that's for sure. Sounds like all of them are. I know Billie that Bitch has lived with more guys and have sex with 80% of Mtn City and Lindsey would say Half of Mtn city Then you Trade and Butler and then you have Doe and then Johnson City and then Kings port she has been all over and she does have HIV this is all around town. and Tara she will give it to anyone her poor Husband he's a nice guy but he never wants to be home with her. I think when his baby is 18 he will leave her dumb ass too. She is a whore too. I agree with you both. and this girl Jenelle I do know as in Passing but she is a good girl and was brought up right you can tell everything is your welcome and Hello and thank you and she just a sweet girl. I will be praying for Jenelle. As far as the other ones go there no good whore sluts and that is carrying something and giving it to everyone. Damn girls. They live in high school still and they need to grow up.

Matt Potter AOL, United States Apr 21, 2010:

Jenelle is a sweet person and ppl try to get her. But she has alot of us behind her if she know's us or not. But Her Dad is Big time and he will deal with the rest of this sh*t. There F**king whores and thats all this town is and Drugs. I know for sure Billie Jean and Lindsey did drugs together and i know Lindsey does Meth she get's off Jason. I know wy to much lol. I love that Jenelle is not like them she stayed sweet . . . . they are dumb ass holes. mother fuckers get what's comeing there way. and they dont know who i am.

Matt Potter AOL, United States Apr 22, 2010:

Well guess Bill dont know that have his Number and his phone is being taped. Ha know what he said about Jenelle and it was wrong. He's a fucking work when these's girls are doing this to Jenelle we got our stuff and Jenelle I'm sure has stuff too. I'm going to be posting numbers if they dont stop buging Jenelle. And then all kind's of ppl will be calling them. I have cell's to home phone numbers. and fucking Billie is geting so fat with that baby she looks like a chipmonk thats eating to many nuts LOL. I hope she lose's that baby in time. It dont need a mother like Billie and Bill he's no father by the way he acts and talks. Sooner thy move out of town the better. I think something about geting a house. I hope he cant get it. I hope they have to live out in the woods. More better for chipmonk, she cant make friends out there and fuck deer and bear and whatever else. I hope a bear would eat her but the way she looks it would go runing the other way LOL. Ugly ass Bitch whore. Cant leave no one alone. Drugie whore ass Bitch. Go fuck a damn tree for all i care. Leave Jenelle alone.

Mike Dunn, United States Apr 22, 2010:

I'm about to fight with you Billie why dont you shut up your fucking moth you Bitch. One day girl you are going to get beat up really good andleft for dead. You better sut up you bitch. Go fuck a cow for all i care. Damn hooker, slut bag whore .... And your Basterd baby take it with you and leave this fucking town. You wont leave here alive.

Matt Potter AOL, United States Apr 22, 2010:

Damn i think we just need to gut her and leave her for dead and kill the damn fucking whore. . . you're a fucking no good person n your day is comeing

---

From the thread "Jenelle Potter strikes again" - after the arrest of Buddy Potter and Jamie Curd - posts presumed to be Jenelle (due to similarities in grammar, punctuation and spelling) hiding under different usernames

Jilly, Mountain City, TN, Jun 12, 2012

Yes and her Family and known Jamie as a baby and it sound's like you need to leave Jenelle alone she has done nothing to anyone. And let me tell you everyone picks on her she moved here and it started but Girls are crazy. She is a the sweet careing on and someone is always trying to tare her down. So if you really don't know her then leave her alone everyone should. Her dumb ass sister Christie is the crazy one for starting the fires and lieing and hurting a lot of people in her life. She need's to deal with her own Isses.

Jilly, Mountain City, TN Jun 12, 2012

Yes is also very sick with so much on the girl and you all think it's funny just wait in time you all will get something and die of something health wise some point no one lives forever. I hope Krama hits all of you. Lindsey and Christie

Jilly, Mountain City, TN Jul 3, 2012

Just Keep on Talking and makeing Jenelle look bad. When None of them did anything. It's a Drug Deal that went Wrong. Can't anyone see this? Well Small town come with small Brains...

Jilly, Mountain City, TN Jul 24, 2012

Guess what Jenelle does not have a Computer and she does not want to get on it. And for your info .. You have no idea what She is even going through or dealing with. SHe is geting rid of her facebook when her lawer want's her too. Now you can think it's her all you want but the poor girl has been very sick and has a lot going on. So what if you were friend you are a backstaber. As i see it you have no clue about anything. She don't care about friends. She has the ones who matter most in PA and we call and talk and we are also down here. So you dont want to start this fucking fight. Her sister is in on this and Lindsey Thomas and her dumb little fucking druggie friends. Words are made up and peolpe can make you do things so dont say they are Guilty . When you have nothing but words. Jenelle is not on this and SHE HAS NO COMPUTER and I cant blame her. YOU AND HER SISTER AND OTHERS are EVIL and You my friend are going to fucking HELL SO go on and stay away from Jenelle Don't call her either. Stay away from her and She almost died over a 3 weeks ago and CPR and coma and ect. I'm not going to put anything else out there. But the cops have the Reports where Jenelle went them Frist. Billie and and Bill Did not. SO there are lies. Your going to Hell with everyone else.

Mike m, United States Sep 25, 2012

Chrisite is the mine issue in her family's life and brings things on her self we know a lot about her she will go down in time

Mean, United States Feb 14, 2013

Jenelle has every right to be in this town she has done nothing but ppl still want to set her for what resin. I don't think anyone did this but for drugs. And she took up for her mom and self and she getting a back bone and there is so much lieing from others trying to hurt her for no reason it will never bring back drug deals back. They will befogtton in time. Buddy Jamie and jenelle and Barbara did nothing wrong. Ppl said that jenelle was to nice and weak and you pick her out because she better then anyone I have met that's I will say. Ask Christie Grover about the drugs and lies and she knows a lot. So go on being mean girls

Mean, United States Feb 14, 2013

Also she has not had a computer for over a year and she has not done nothing to do with anyone. But her family so grow up little mtn city.

A BLUEGRASS TRAGEDY

THE STOCKDALE FAMILY MURDERS

1

MURDER ON THE FARM

On Thursday, June 15, 2017, at 4:31 p.m., Stark County, Ohio, police received a 911 emergency call from a nearby location. The call had come from a landline, but the caller had hung up without saying anything. When the emergency dispatcher was unable to reach anyone by calling the number back, they notified the police station closest to where the call came from.

Storms were brewing, making phone coverage patchy, when Sheriff George T. Maier sent two deputies to check that everything was okay. Not overly concerned, the officers drove through the picturesque hills, past sprawling farms, to the location of the call, which they had traced to an address on Dolphin Street in Bolivar, a quaint town in the north-east of the state. With a population of less than 1,000 people, Bolivar boasted a mix between rustic, small-town life and suburban life. It was the sort of place where neighbors were friendly but not overly involved with each other's business and many folks aimed for a self-sufficient lifestyle.

The property the officers were heading to was in the

more rural part of Bolivar, a small farm situated down a private laneway at 9115 Dolphin Street. The house was set back around 200 yards from the road, down a driveway lined with pasture fencing that kept the animals contained and electric fencing to keep the groundhogs out. As they got closer, a single gunshot rang out from inside the house. The officers took cover and immediately called for backup. They could see that the front door was open, and it appeared that someone was lying on the floor.

When it was deemed safe, police officers carefully entered the home. Inside, they found blood, three members of one family in a scene of unthinkable brutality.

———

That night, a small crowd gathered at the Amish County Theater in Walnut Creek expecting to hear the Stockdale Family Band play. The Stockdales were minor celebrities in the area. Several years earlier, they had featured on the reality TV show *Wife Swap*. The mother, Kathy, had swapped places with a city-based woman for two weeks, contrasting a conservative rural lifestyle with a liberal urban one. Kathy's husband, Tim, and their four sons had formed a successful bluegrass band that had toured all over the country. Kathy was the band manager and publicist.

By this time, only the two youngest sons—Jacob and James—still played alongside their father, Tim. Their two older brothers had moved away to pursue careers in more populated cities in Michigan and Philadelphia with their young families. The remaining Stockdales were the regular house band at the Walnut Creek Theater, and they always drew an appreciative crowd, especially the star attraction, award-winning 25-year-old fiddle player Jacob Stockdale.

But there was no performance that night. The Stockdale Family Band would never play again.

2

A HARD LIFE, BUT A GOOD LIFE

Tim and Kathy Stockdale met in the early 1980s at Ohio State University, where they were studying for agriculture degrees and were both members of the university's agronomy club . They were kindred spirits, both adhering to conservative fundamentalist Christian values and a desire to live a simple, hardworking, and pure life. They also shared a love of Christian music. Tim had played rhythm guitar since he was young, entertaining his family around the campfire with his skill and bluesy singing voice. Kathy didn't play an instrument, but she appreciated the music and was supportive of Tim's hobby, pleased that he only played gospel and other wholesome tunes with no swearing or inappropriate lyrics.

Neither Tim nor Kathy believed in dating unless there was a clear and intended path to marriage. They married on August 10, 1985, and their first son, Calvin, came along a couple of years later. Charles followed two years later, then Jacob another two years after that. The baby of the family, James, was born in 1996. The couple embraced traditional roles in their marriage, with Tim going out to earn a living while Kathy stayed at home to take care of the cooking, cleaning, and raising the children.

With four young boys, Tim and Kathy grew increasingly concerned about the effects of urban living on their family. They wanted to shield their boys from the "violent language, sexual influences, drinking, smoking, drugs, and rap music" that they believed ran rampant in the city. Eschewing traditional education, Kathy home-schooled her sons in an effort to "keep their minds pure and their bodies healthy and keep out the influences of modern society." From a very early age, the boys were given age-appropriate chores around the home, and were banned from watching television, instead being given instruments to learn. Leisure time meant reading approved books or playing music with the family.

It had always been Tim and Kathy's dream to move to a rural area and raise their boys on a farm, protected from negative outside influences. Their search took them to a 150-year-old farm in Bolivar, Ohio. It was a small town, but one that was just a short drive from historic attractions, such as the picturesque Zoar village, which hosted reenactments of German separatists escaping religious persecution in their homeland in the 1800s, and Fort Laurens, a historical fort from the Civil War era. Kathy and Tim thought the small farm ideal to realize their desire to be completely self-sufficient, raising or growing their own food in a free-range, organic environment, free from steroids or antibiotics, and to raise healthy, hardworking, and God-fearing sons. The Stockdale family moved there in 1999 when their oldest son, Calvin, was eleven and their youngest, James, was two. "The day we moved, we heard gunshots in our neighborhood, and I knew we made the right decision," Tim later said.

One of the first tasks they had was to find a church that resonated with their beliefs. The Zion Reformed Church, part of an ultra-conservative breakaway Presbyterian church, in Winesburg, fit the bill. Its pamphlet claimed:

> We believe that man should live according to the moral standards set forth in Scripture. This includes: living a holy life; being full of love, joy, peace, longsuffering, gentleness, goodness, faith, meekness, and temperance. Therefore, we are opposed to: adultery, fornication, uncleanness (including sodomy, lesbianism, bisexuality, bestiality, incest, pornography, and other forms of moral impurity), lasciviousness, idolatry, witchcraft, hatred, variance, emulations, wrath, strife, seditions, heresies, envyings, murders (including abortion and euthanasia), drunkenness, and revelings.

Zion Reformed became the Stockdale family church.

The family became very insular. The boys' days were structured by their parents from the moment they got up in the morning until the time they went to bed and they rarely left the property. "Everything they need is here on the farm with their family," Kathy claimed.

They set about raising chickens, both for laying and for food, as well as cows and pigs for beef and pork. It was important to Tim and Kathy to know exactly how their food was raised and "to eat close to the land and to regain our health." Anything that they didn't grow or raise themselves, they bought from or traded with other local organic farms. Processed food was banned from the house altogether. Kathy called such foods 'Frankenfoods', believing them to be science experiments gone wrong. "It is not real food for real people," she said.

The Stockdales did not have a lot of money and although they sold what was left over of their produce, it was not enough to cover their expenses, so Tim still had to attend a full-time job delivering animal nutrients to farms across the state. Kathy dedicated herself completely to her children, ensuring that the boys knew what they were supposed to be doing every minute of the day. They did a couple of hours of schoolwork in the morning, and Kathy drummed into them that failure was not an option. The rest of the day was taken up with chores around the house and farm. If they carried out their chores well, they received tokens, with an extra token for displaying the right attitude and "a glad heart." The tokens could be traded for privileges, such as listening to a radio show or a stick of gum.

The boys were on a strict diet that included no sugar, wheat or junk food. Each night, Kathy insisted the boys drink a spoonful of cod-liver oil. She said that it kept their heart, bones, and brain healthy. Later, Kathy insisted the family follow the "leaky gut" diet. Leaky gut syndrome is a controversial digestive condition in which bacteria and toxins "leak" through the intestinal wall, but it is not generally recognized by mainstream medical professionals as a real condition. The diet the boys had to follow consisted of fibrous and fermented vegetables, fruits, cultured dairy products, healthy fats, and lean, unprocessed pasture-raised meats.

The boysencouraged each other to be healthy. One family friend noted that when the boys joined kids who ate a more conventional diet, although they were happy to share, they always turned down things made with sugar or processed foods. If the boys come home with candy that someone had given them, Kathy would buy it off them with tokens and then throw it away.

Tim and Kathy valued a good work ethic—Kathy was proud that she could gut and clean a chicken in under four minutes—and they were determined to instill their values on their children. "No one in this family gets a free ride," Kathy would say. "The boys have to learn that the only way to succeed is by working." As the boys grew up, their responsibilities around the house and farm grew with them. By the time the youngest, James, was ten years old, he was responsible for cleaning the bathroom and doing the breakfast dishes before home-school, then vacuuming and dusting, watering the garden and sweeping the porch in the afternoon and clearing the dishes after dinner. His older brothers had even more to do, with Calvin and Charles taking on the heavier tasks around the farm. Jacob was completely responsible for the large brood of chickens, feeding them, mucking them out and getting them back into their pens in the evening, ensuring they were safe from the foxes that prowled at night. The chickens weren't pets, though, and Jacob was also responsible, when the time came, for killing them to feed the family.

"It might be a hard life, but it's a good life," Tim and Kathy said to each other. It became the family motto.

3

THE STOCKDALE FAMILY BAND

The Stockdale children were not allowed television or video games, or to have unsupervised play with other children. The family had an internet connection, but the boys could only use it if they had an educational purpose and a destination to go to, and once that was fulfilled, they were to log off immediately. They were not encouraged to play sports because of the competitive nature of team games. "The glory seeking can encourage too much of a self centered aspect that is not desirable in clean living children," Kathy said. As the older boys became young men, they were forbidden from dating until they were ready for marriage.

There were few reasons for the boys to leave the farm. They attended church, music lessons, scouts and debating club with other home-schooled children. Charles and Jacob also attended woodworking class once a week, as their parents thought it a practical skill. The boys were expected to make their own money, so they sold chickens and worked on other farms during the summer. The money they made was used to pay for their own music lessons and debating classes, or to pay fines for being late to breakfast or other infractions of the rules.

Kathy Stockdale was determined to choose a lifestyle that allowed her children to spend most of their time with the family. She wanted them to work together, sing together, pray together, eat together, and play together. Their entertainment consisted of listening to Christian radio programming or attending a pre-vetted movie (provided the boys had earned enough tokens from their chores for the privilege), reading approved books and playing music.

Music was the glue that kept the Stockdale family together. Some nights, Tim played guitar and the kids pulled out pots and pans and kept the rhythm. As they got older, the boys began to learn a variety of instruments, and music practice became an essential part of every day.

Tim's preference was for gospel, Christian bluegrass, and country tunes, and as the boys grew more proficient, they began to call themselves the Stockdale Family Band. The band became the focus of the family. Tim played rhythm guitar and Calvin, the oldest of the boys, was proficient in several instruments but specialized in the banjo. He was the band's front man and lead vocalist in the early days. Charles played guitar and mandolin and helped out on vocals. James learned rhythm and timing on a bucket bass—a five-gallon bucket, a broomstick handle, and a string—before graduating to an upright bass. He was also an enthusiastic and natural performer who enjoyed front-man duties. All the boys played multiple instruments, but Jacob was the most talented musician of them all.

Jacob played fiddle, and while the other members of the band practiced hard and played well because of it, Jacob was a natural and completely devoted to his instrument. After learning the foundations of classical violin using the Suzuki method (which relies mostly on sound rather than reading sheet music) at the age of seven, he soon began improvising, coming up with his own unique sound, a mix of bluegrass and Ohio old-time fiddling styles. His parents began entering him into competitions at a very early age, and by the time he was thirteen he had won five old-time fiddle contests, including the State of Ohio Youth Fiddle Championship. Jacob had high standards for both himself and his brothers, and his attention to detail and exacting standards kept the whole band on their toes.

The boys were still young when the band began getting gigs. The five-piece band comprised guitar, fiddle, mandolin, banjo and bass, with alternating lead vocalists. At first, they played for family and friends at parties and gatherings, but then they started getting booked for church events. Their high-energy and fun routines made them crowd favorites and word of their performances spread through the community. People couldn't get enough of their energetic upbeat gospel music, made for foot-stomping and barn dancing. They incorporated three and four-part harmonies, comedy, trick instrumentation and clog dancing in their routines. They often opened a performance with the song "Country Life," which started with the family's motto: "Well it's a hard life, but it's a good, good life."

Kathy was the band's manager, booking gigs, negotiating fees and managing the finances. A bit of a self-proclaimed control freak, this was a role in which she excelled. To make sure the boys stayed on track, she put up lyrics for songs they needed to rehearse in the bathroom. She started a website, stockdalefamilyband.com, to provide updates about the family and invited interested parties to book gigs. She targeted the pastors of local churches to book the Stockdale Family Band, writing:

Dear Pastor

Thank you for interest in our ministry! As a Christian family, we are happy to serve many different denominations.

Our goals are to:

1) Serve you in this music ministry.

2) Successfully gain the attendance of your church and community.

3) Secure the means to continue with this ministry.

We provide Christian and family friendly entertainment— such as a Gospel music concert, Bluegrass and Gospel, comedy, etc.—We negotiate a fee to come. There are some entertainment events that may be conducted on a love offering basis. Contact us for clarification.

Thank you again for expressing interest in our ministry. We hope to be able to meet your needs and build lasting relationships that glorify the Lord Jesus Christ.

The calls trickled in, and the band began to play more regularly, gaining a few more fans at each gig. Eventually, the calls became a deluge, and by 2007, the Stockdale Family Band didn't have a single weekend when they weren't playing somewhere. Then, in April 2007, a call came that was far different from any that Kathy had received before. It was from the ABC, one of the largest television broadcasters in the country. They said they were looking for a family bluegrass band to feature on a popular reality TV show and that the Stockdale Family Band had come highly recommended.

The show's name was *Wife Swap*.

4

THE WIFE SWAP EXPERIENCE

Wife Swap is a long-running TV show that started in the United Kingdom, but which has since franchised out to several countries, including the United States. The premise of the show is that the wives and mothers of two radically different families swap places for two weeks. During the first week, the wives must follow the rules of the family they have been swapped into. In the second week, the family must follow the rules instituted by the new wife. At the end of two weeks, the couples come together to discuss what they have learned from each other's lifestyles.

Although it is pitched as a social experiment, Wife Swap is first and foremost entertainment. To ramp up the drama as much as possible, the producers pair participants with families from thoroughly different backgrounds and with divergent values and lifestyles. They may swap a wife from a vegan household with one from a family of hunters, a homophobe with one half of a gay couple, put a neat freak into a messy household or swap an affluent wife with a struggling one. Strict parents are swapped with those who spoil their kids rotten and fitness fanatics with those who prefer a wholly unhealthy lifestyle. In one episode, a professional organizer swapped places with a woman who "embraced a pirate lifestyle." In another, a high-flying corporate executive found herself swapped to a family that lived on a boat without electricity or running water, and who shared one towel between them all.

Not surprisingly, the exchange of wives from couples who are often polar opposites has led to the show's fair share of scandals. An Oklahoma man sued the show for misrepresentation and distress when his "wife" turned out to be a gay man. A man on the UK version of the show committed suicide after being humiliated when his sexual practices were made public. A participant who lost his job and received death threats after being labeled "the worst husband in America" accused the producers of manufacturing a character for him to play. He claimed that, under duress of constant cameras and the threat that he was not being entertaining enough, they persuaded him to amp up his hostility toward his swapped wife. Another participant, who was a teenager when her show aired, sued the show, claiming that she was represented in such a false light on air that she suffered bullying at school that ruined her confidence. The lawsuit was settled for an undisclosed sum.

Perhaps the most famous scandal to arise in relation to a *Wife Swap* family was that of "Balloon Boy." The Heene family were depicted as chaotic storm chasers who were swapped with a serene and safety-conscious family. The Heenes made great television and were invited back as fan favorites for *Wife Swap*'s 100th episode.

While in negotiations for another TV show, Richard and Mayumi Heene contacted authorities in a panic. They claimed they had released a homemade helium-filled gas balloon that was shaped like a flying saucer into the atmosphere near their home in Colorado and they believed their six-year-old son was trapped inside. News crews descended on the family and they were soon a worldwide media phenomenon. People around the globe watched the live feed of the balloon's path with bated breath. The National Guard was brought in, and helicopters set off in pursuit of the balloon, hoping to retrieve it and bring the boy to safety.

When the balloon landed about twelve miles from Denver International Airport, the police found no sign of the boy. News soon began to spread that an object had been seen falling from the balloon, sparking an urgent search. Later that day, the little boy was found hiding in the attic of his own home. He had apparently been there the entire time. The entire episode was strongly suspected to be a publicity stunt dreamed up by his fame-hungry parents who were hoping to get their own reality TV show. Richard Heene always maintained that it was an accident. Their new reality show never got made.

For the US version of *Wife Swap*, potential families could live anywhere in the United States, but had to consist of two parents with at least two children over the age of five living at home. *Wife Swap* advertised for participants in all manner of media, on Craigslist and through niche hobby websites. Most people featured on the show applied after seeing one of these advertisements. However, sometimes producers were looking for a specific type of family and recruiters would approach suitable families directly. This is what happened with the Stockdale Family, who otherwise were unlikely to have ever heard of the TV show.

When the ABC producer contacted Kathy Stockdale

about putting her family on *Wife Swap*, she told them that she wasn't interested, pointing out that the family didn't even have a television. Rather than putting them off, this revelation simply piqued the producers' interest further and they insisted that she talk it over with the family. She was told she would trade places with a mother from an urban family to juxtapose with their rural lifestyle.

Tim was not keen, but the four boys, by now aged eleven to nineteen, were enthusiastic. Kathy and Tim had to admit that the money would come in handy. Despite the family's hard work and efforts, the farm was not self-sustaining, and Tim continued to take on extra work outside the home, which took him away from his family more often than either of them liked. The compensation for being on *Wife Swap*, especially in the case of being approached rather than applying, was significant. The Stockdale family had the potential to earn $20,000 for two weeks' work.

After much family discussion and a careful read through of the twenty-page contract, Kathy and Tim decided that accepting the ABC's offer would provide a unique learning experience for the family. With a mix of trepidation and excitement, they signed the contract to appear on the TV show, where Kathy would switch places for two weeks with the matriarch of another family. She would have no idea who the other family were until the show went into production.

F ilming of *Wife Swap* was set to take place three months later, in July 2007. First, producers worked with the Stockdale family to get them ready for the intense production schedule. One of the pivotal moments in the show is the exchange of the "family manual," supposedly penned by the wife of the family. In reality, the manual is put together by the producers after a three-day interview with the family. The manual reflected the values and practices of the family, but perhaps played up the extremes of both.

The producers also worked with the family to decide which events would take place during the filming, so that the swapped wife could get an idea of the lifestyle of her new family. Although the show claims that the wives will live by their new family's rules for the "first week" and then implement rule changes that the new family must abide by in the "second week," the whole thing is filmed over a period of six to seven days, for twelve to fourteen hours per day. The Stockdale family would have to squeeze in all the tasks required on the farm that would normally be done over a longer period, as well as a musical gig, into the first few days of the schedule. They did not know what they would be doing for the final three days, when the swapped wife's "new rules" were being implemented.

Once the preliminaries were arranged, a nervous Kathy left her family for longer than they had ever been separated before. She traveled 400 miles to a house in Poplar Grove, in Boone County, northern Illinois. It was not exactly a big city, but the house was in an urban area, with neighbors nearby. As was the format of the show, before she met her "swap family," Kathy let herself in to look around the house she was to live in for the next two weeks and to read the family manual that had been left for her by the woman with whom she had swapped lives, Laurie Tonkovic.

Wandering around, Kathy noted that the house seemed a little chaotic, with clothes, half-eaten food and other mess allowed to pile up. She was confronted by a used ashtray, something she hadn't seen for a long time, and female apparel in a boy's bedroom, which she claimed confused her. She found the Tonkovic family manual in the kitchen and began to read about the type of family she had been swapped into.

———

U nlike the Stockdales, but like most other participants, the Tonkovics responded to an advertisement inviting applications by families who wanted to be featured on the show. Laurie thought she had a lot to teach another family and was open to growing and learning herself. It wasn't her first television appearance. She had appeared on Oprah's talk show when she had been living in Chicago over a decade earlier, in an episode about feuding neighbors.

"Everybody knows when the Tonkovics are throwing a party, we can have 150 kids out here; dancing, laughing, hooking up, fooling around together," Kathy read. She had assumed that she would be entering a family with young children whom she could relate to, and hopefully educate a little. Instead, she discovered from the manual, she would be living with 52-year-old John, 21-year-old Paul and 17-year-old Meghan. Reading a little further, she was shocked to discover Paul's girlfriend, Samantha, and Meghan's boyfriend, Hector also lived in the house.

As she read on, it became clear that the family she had swapped into was the antithesis to her own, in terms of values and practices. "The sanctity of marriage is not a value," Kathy noted grimly. This did not sit well with the teachings of her religion: "God intends sexual intimacy to only occur between a man and a woman who are married to each other ... God has commanded that no intimate sexual activity be engaged in outside of a marriage between a man and a woman."

The manual explained the mess that Kathy had walked into, Laurie stating, "It takes a lot of garbage or dishes to pile up before someone takes the initiative around here. Our theory is, if you can stick your mess on the pile without anything falling off, you're good!" Dinner dishes were left in the sink overnight before Laurie might—or might not—wash them the next day. None of the kids had jobs—they came to Laurie for anything they wanted. As Kathy said to the camera, "It sounds like we have adults mooching off of this household."

Once she had time to digest the manual, Kathy met her swap family—husband John, kids Paul and Meghan, and their partners. She soon discovered that 21-year-old Paul aspired to become a rapper and that he wrote songs about sex, violence, and current affairs, all with graphic language. None of the younger generation were required to do any chores, or even clean up after themselves. "My 11-year-old is more mature than Paul," Kathy noted to the camera.

For the next three days, the families were filmed for up to fourteen hours a day, going about an accelerated version of their normal life. The Tonkovics threw one of their famous backyard parties, with Paul rapping and partygoers dancing suggestively, much to the horror of Kathy, who declared it "Foul. Shameful. Disgusting."

The Tonkovic family found Kathy extremely judgmental. She accused John of bad parenting and not providing any guidance for his kids, of preferring to be their friend rather than their father. Confronting John about the children, including those that weren't his own, not working, not contributing around the house, and taking money whenever they want, he told her "As a family, we live for today. Because if the Man Upstairs decides he needs some angels, there might not be a tomorrow."

M eanwhile, in Ohio, Laurie was observing the Stockdale family routine. She had experienced a similar culture shock and was discovering a very different way of life, in a family where TV and video games were banned, prayer was sung around the table, and the children's time was structured from morning until night. She didn't think that the controlled environment was healthy. "They were almost robotic," Laurie said of the boys on the first day as they did their chores. "They just jump into gear and know what to do and, boom boom, they do it."

"It's nice because I know what I have to do next," James told Laurie when she quizzed him on how he felt about the structure in his day.

The Stockdale Family Band took Laurie to one of their gigs at the local hall. She wasn't impressed with the old-fashioned, wholesome music, declaring that she thought it belonged to the father, Tim, rather than being what the boys really wanted to play.

She quizzed 16-year-old Charles about whether he was interested in dating, and he told her that he thought it better to wait until he was ready to settle down and start a family. Laurie wondered how he would ever find someone to marry if he wasn't allowed to date and wondered whether the family believed in arranged marriages.

Laurie found the Stockdales' way of life stifling and wept for the boys whose childhoods she believed had been stolen from them. Her attempts to speak to Tim were quickly shut down and he would not entertain any suggestions that he give his sons some more freedom. "I'm not letting the world dictate to me how to raise my kids," he told her.

I n the second half of the week, the show depicts the wives coming up with the new rules that the families must follow. Like the family manual, in reality, it is the producers who come up with them. The new wife must instigate these new rules—purported to be hers—into the family.

"Tonkovics," Kathy declared, "It's time someone turned you into a wholesome family." Kathy's rules included disconnecting the TV and getting rid of the video games, to be replaced by "good hard work" in order to receive money. John was to learn how to provide discipline to his kids and guidance for their future. She told the family they had to throw an old-fashioned barn dance and Paul was to write a song with no swearing in his lyrics. The girls had to take care of Baby Think It Over dolls that cried whenever their needs were not being fulfilled, to teach them about unplanned pregnancies. She brought a priest in and demanded that the young couples get married. When they refused, she told them that they would not be allowed to share a room with their partners for the remainder of filming.

Back at the Stockdale farm, Laurie told her swap family that she had brought in cable TV, video games and that they were not to do any chores—their father Tim would have to do them all. She swapped out their natural organic diet for frozen pizzas and other pre-packaged food. The boys were to write a rap song and have a "rap off" with established performers. Most controversially, Laurie told the two older

boys, Calvin and Charles, that they were to invite girls out
on a date. Tim was furiously against this.

Calvin and Charles were also very much against it.
Calvin took Laurie outside and told her politely, but firmly,
that he didn't like being forced to do something he didn't
want to do. He told her he was afraid of what her rules were
doing emotionally to his younger brothers. As he pleaded
his case with Laurie, tears welled up in his eyes and fell
down his cheeks.

Similarly, 15-year-old Jacob "freaked out" about the free-
doms Laurie was offering, in particular television and video
games. She claimed that he tearfully told her he was terrified his religious parents would be mad and he would "burn
in hell."

Although participants had been known to veto rules on
occasion, they were bound by the contracts they signed not
to rock the boat too much. If they made too much trouble
for the producers, they would lose any compensation
promised to them. If a participant refused to go any further
and stopped filming, they could be liable to pay back any
production expenses already incurred. In one infamous
interview, a participant alleged he was told that if he didn't
comply with the show, his wife would remain stranded on
the other side of the country and the production company
would not pay for her return. Another disgruntled former
contestant claimed she was threatened with a $5 million fine
for breach of contract.

Laurie (or more likely, the producers) got their way. The
Stockdale boys played video games while their father did all
the chores. "It's fun for the present," Jacob said of playing
the games. "But it has no real value."

James chimed in, "I feel guilty right now, but I love it!"

Tim was not impressed. "I believe my children are

becoming mind-numbed robots," he said, "totally oblivious to everything that's going on."

Tim was similarly against every fun initiative Laurie tried to implement for the boys. "Everything is an obstacle," Laurie said.

The older boys were still totally opposed to going out on a date, but Laurie was adamant and asked them where they would like to go. "You obviously know we don't go out," said Charles, much to Laurie's disbelief.

"Going out has certain connotations," Calvin agreed.

"I understand that's how you were raised," Laurie said.

"I would appreciate you keeping my parents out, because that's *my* decision," Calvin told her firmly.

Once again, Laurie (or production) eventually won out, reframing the event as "just hanging out," and the boys went out on a double date. It is unclear who the teenage girls were, as Calvin was shown making a call to set the date up, but then the two girls introduced themselves to the boys when they arrived for dinner as though they had never met. Conversation began awkwardly, but soon moved into more comfortable territory when they talked about music.

Afterwards, Calvin deemed the date a lot of fun, saying it was enjoyable to hang out with members of the opposite sex, and told Tim he would like to do it again. Tim responded only with, "We'll see."

The one time all the boys and Tim showed great enthusiasm was when it came to writing and performing their own rap song. They admitted that they had written very little of their own work and they discovered they had a talent for it, Tim even coming up with a stanza of rhyming lyrics. They put it to music and declared they had invented a new musical genre: rapgrass.

At the end of the experiment, the two couples met up in

what became a fiery showdown. John Tonkovic told Kathy that he felt she was extremely judgmental and disrespectful to his family and Laurie jumped in to defend her husband and kids. As Laurie stormed out of the meeting, she said to Tim, "I really enjoyed you and your children, but YOU?" She jabbed a finger at Kathy. "If you have anything else to say about my family, keep it to yourself."

5

LIFE AFTER WIFE SWAP AND GROWING MUSIC FAME

With filming finished and several months to wait until their program aired, little changed with the Stockdale family's way of life, although pre-approved video games were introduced into the reward system. Tim and Kathy's views on dating had not changed, however, with Calvin confirming, "There was no second date."

The band continued to grow and thrive, now adding original songs to the repertoire. They went on regular tours, playing at fairs and in competitions, many of which they won with their multi-instrument talents. The Amish County Theater in Walnut Creek provided them with a residency and their lively music, and comedic farm tales complemented the comedy acts that were popular in the area. A portion of all proceeds of their ticket sales went to charity, such as to support persecuted Christians in Iraq.

Kathy continued to manage the band or, as one acquaintance put it, micromanage the band. "I spoke with Kathy at a festival for a while," she said, "and micromanaging does not even come close to describing it. I do not think there is an

English word to describe the micromanaging and oppression."

While all the male members of the family had musical talent, it was Jacob's star that continued to surpass that of his father and brothers. Although he played multiple instruments, it was on the fiddle that he truly shined. In 2007/08 he was awarded an Ohio Arts Council Traditional Arts Apprenticeship to learn Ohio-style fiddling under master fiddler Adam Jackson, and branched out to record an instrumental solo CD, *An Ohio Tradition*. For his brothers, the band was a fun way to earn a little money, but for Jacob, music was his life.

T he Wife Swap episode featuring the Stockdale and Tonkavic families aired in the US in April 2008.

In the lead up to the show airing, participants were contacted to provide quotes to newspapers for publicity. "Being a farm, home-schooling, bluegrass band family, we enjoy a lot of common experiences, but we have to chalk the Wife Swap adventure as the grand family bonding experience for the Stockdales for which we will never be the same," Kathy Stockdale told *Bluegrass Today*. "We relate differently in that we have even more and deeper collective experiences where we overcame obstacles and accomplished a giant task together. No one else will understand the Wife Swap journey like we do and that is one of the things that will make our family unit different and special forever."

When asked if she would do it again, Kathy responded, "Would I go through junior high school again? Would I endure childbirth again? Would I play Monopoly for a second round? Aaaaaa—no. Each one of these experiences is worthwhile and so was Wife Swap, but I accomplished what I set out to do the first time."

Laurie Tonkovic told a reporter that she had seen the episode a month previously and said the TV crews captured her true personality. "It's totally me, 100 per cent," she said. "I thought it turned out great and I have no regrets."

It is possible that both the Stockdale and Tonkovic families saw a different version of the episode to each other, and different to that which went to air. One former Wife Swap participant claimed contestants were shown a version of the episode before it screened that was skewed to show that contestant and their family in a more complimentary light. She said, "They showed us the 'final cut' and it showed us in a more favorable way than the actual final edit did. So, we saw the episode they showed us and invited a bunch of people over to watch. Then what aired wasn't at all like what they showed us. That was pretty shady."

It is likely that neither the Stockdales' nor the Tonkovics' lifestyles were as extreme as were depicted on the Wife Swap episode that went to air. The producers arrived at the families' houses with an idea of how they want the family to be portrayed, and although the show was not scripted, the scenarios they put them in and the rule changes were designed to provoke a reaction that fit within the narrative. With over 100 hours of filming, and only half an hour making it to air, there are many ways of using footage to shape a story. Scenes may be run out of order, conversations provided out of context and when a participant hasn't made a statement the producers want to hear, sometimes they resort to "Frankenbites," which are soundbites from different sentences spliced together.

The oldest boy, Calvin Stockdale, for example, was

already away at college and had a Facebook account as early as March 2007—a month before filming began. Watching the episode, viewers were led to believe he still lived full time on the farm under the iron thumb of his parents, oblivious to social media. However, there is little recourse for reality participants who think the way they are depicted amounts to fiction. The thick stack of waivers and confidentiality agreements they sign before filming starts usually has a clause that expressly permits the producers to do just that.

Some people are happy with how they are portrayed but many are not, especially when viewer sentiment is not on their side. Some take to the internet to voice their fury at how they are treated. One former participant, Kate Martinez, blogged:

> In December of 2006, my family was asked to participate in an episode of "Wife Swap." We thought it would be the chance of a lifetime to get 20K and get to experience "living in somebody elses shoes." However as soon as they showed up to start shooting; props, scripts, and scenes in tow, we became nervous about what we signed up for.
>
> The quote "Believe nothing you read, and only half of what you see" should be the motto for "reality television." The show couldnt be a bigger load of crap. It claims to be shot over two weeks when in reality it is shot over one. They rearrange your house to make your family come across a certain way, they "black out" windows to "shoot a night scene" or bring huge lights outside if its night and they need to shoot a "day scene." They come to your house with props, a SCRIPT, a list of SCENES to shoot, THEY WRITE the manuals, THEY WRITE the "rule changes." The families depicted on the show are more like puppets asked to do and say whatever the production demands and if they dont, ultimately they will be sued for 5

MILLION DOLLARS. Some people that do these kinds of shows dont mind. Some people go on the show, ham it up, do whatever the producers tell them to do because they dont care and they want to "be famous." However those that offer resistance quickly get assigned the role of the "bad guys"; and THAT is what happened to my family.

In short, I deeply regret doing the show—it was nothing that I thought it would be and no amount of money in the world is worth that world believing a lie about your family. I would strongly advise anybody considering doing the show to reconsider and think about what is really important to them.

On social media, there was significant backlash against the Stockdale parents. Viewers were aghast at how strict Kathy and Tim were, with many claiming the way they were raising their boys was tantamount to child abuse. Kathy was considered a judgmental control freak ruled by religious zealotry. Fortunately, the younger boys were most likely shielded from most of the criticism due to their limited access to the internet.

It wasn't only the Stockdale family who came under fire. The Tonkovics also received their fair share of criticism from the public, much of which Laurie Tonkovic felt was undeserved. She was also unprepared for the hateful emails and social media messages sent to her and her family. It didn't stop her from applying to have her family feature on the show again for *Wife Swap*'s 100th episode in 2008, however. "We never claim to be perfect, but we love each other, and we support each other in everything we do," Laurie told reporters about her bid to take part again. "I want to show them that. I want to show them they were wrong about us."

Regardless of the reception, the Stockdale family's

reality TV appearance provided the band with an extra level of fame and notoriety, and upcoming gigs were often advertised with "as seen on Wife Swap." Kathy Stockdale embraced the extra publicity. In August 2008 she encouraged people who missed the show to tune in, writing on her blog:

> *Dear Friends of the Stockdale Family Band, If you missed it the first time, here's a second chance to see the Stockdale's in their debut television performance and drama. Yes, DRAMA and a little bit of performance on the ABC Wife Swap Stockdale/Tonkavic episode, which airs Wednesday, September 3. Check local listings.*

Local website Canton Repository News regularly reported on the band's rising profile. In June 2008 the website featured a Stockdale Family Band promo video in which the family enthused about making music together. Tim said, "Words can hardly express the joy I feel when I'm on stage and getting the chance to play with some really great musicians and I even get to call them my sons."

A barefoot Jacob said, "Being in the band with my brothers, it's a lot of fun going to different shows and getting to go to different places. It's almost like we get to go on a vacation whenever we go play a show. It's fun and enjoyable." Then to an undisclosed question he grinned sheepishly and said, "I don't know what else to say about that."

Tim finished the video saying, "I count it a real privilege to be able to play with them and the fact that they let me play with them. It's a lot of fun to play with my boys. I think we're making memories for a lifetime."

The band even incorporated the rap song that they wrote for Wife Swap into their shows. The song was called

"Bluegrass Rap" and they coined the name "rapgrass" for the genre. Part of the song went as follows:

We used to live in the city
With the shootin' and the killin'
Now we're in the country
And we're just a chillin'

We're out here in the country
And there's killin' goin' on
But it's all about chickens
Out here on the farm

6

THE STOCKDALE BROTHERS

The band continued to go from strength to strength. Their enthusiasm was infectious, and they gained fans everywhere they played. Calvin was away at Hillsdale College in Michigan, a conservative private college that catered to fundamentalists and homeschoolers, where he was studying for a degree in history. This meant most gigs were done without him, though he joined the band on holidays. As well as their regular gig at the Amish County Theater, the Stockdale Family Band became an integral part of the Stark County Fair, making several appearances over the years. Although most of their gigs were in Ohio, they also traveled to play in the surrounding states: Indiana, Michigan, Kentucky, and Pennsylvania. The band played a lot of community concert series, churches, theaters, and county fairs.

Kathy reveled in her role as manager and created a YouTube channel that showcased the band's performances. She organized the recording of CDs and publicity for the band, which were well received. "The Stockdale Family Band's bluegrass and gospel music is upbeat, down-home and steeped in Americana," wrote one reporter. "It's hard to not smile and tap your feet at the Stockdale's energetic musicianship and enthusiastic show-manship. The love of playing and harmonizing together by these four brothers and their dad is obvious." Tim Stock-dale opened a Facebook account in December 2008, a few months after the airing of Wife Swap, posting videos of their performances.

Despite the depiction of a sheltered, tough life on the reality TV show, the Stockdale boys seemed to have a whole-some and happy childhood. Winters saw them skating and playing hockey on the weekends, followed by parties involving hot meal potlucks and musical jam sessions. When Calvin went off to college, he was interviewed in a local paper and had fond memories of the family home. "I was eleven when we first moved down here. It was amaz-ing," he said. "We built forts, had a pond for swimming in the summer, and ice skating and hockey in the winter. It's great fun. You can hike around all day."

In 2010, second-eldest Charles also left for Hillsdale College to complete a Bachelor of Science, researching the effects of ethanol and taurine in the livers of chick embryos. The four-hour drive meant he no longer lived at home full time, although he was still expected to join the band during school vacations and special weekend occasions. Kathy put a brave face on it, writing in her blog:

The guys who are left: Jacob, James and Tim (Dad) will be recreating themselves and at times will bring a guest banjo player of the week! We don't know exactly, but did you ever wonder what the band was like in the early years? When James played the bucket bass and Charles tried to think what to say next? Well, here is your chance to be part of the change from the

ground up. The wild card is where will Calvin be? Stay tuned
for the Stockdale Family Band Recreated.

She soon found out where Calvin would be. Later that year, Calvin got engaged, began a job at the Institutional Advancement Department of Hillsdale College, and moved out of the family home completely, getting his own place in Michigan which he shared with his bride. They tied the knot in 2011.

With the two older brothers gone, the family brought in Joe Steiner, a banjo and harmonica player from Findlay, Ohio, to play with the band for professional gigs. Joe didn't wear the family uniform, but he and Jacob fed off each other, playing fast-paced dueling banjo and fiddle, which soon became a highlight at the end of the band's performances.

As the older brothers got busier with their own lives and could no longer commit to playing all the time, Jacob and James sometimes performed as a duet, rebranded as the Stockdale Brothers. Kathy uploaded some of their performances to YouTube. The two brothers worked well together, and looked comfortable and happy playing off against each other. James often took the lead, talking to the camera before they launched into one cover or another. Jacob came across as the more sensitive of the two, with a more serious personality. His younger brother enjoyed taking on the persona of the family clown.

James might have been the mouth and confidence of the duo, but it was Jacob who had the most musical talent. He continued to accumulate prizes and accolades for his fiddle playing.

2014 was a momentous year for the Stockdale family. The Stockdale Family Band, minus Calvin, won first place in the Heights Got Talent Contest in Cleveland Heights, on Charles's twenty-fourth birthday. In their signature tan pants, blue shirts and cowboy hats, the band put in a high-energy performance of rollicking bluegrass music, with Jacob on lead vocals. It contained a heavy dose of comedy too, with Tim, Charles and James suddenly swapping instruments mid-song, tossing them to each other and deftly taking up where the other left off. Mostly, though, the five-minute performance showcased the extraordinary talent of Jacob on the fiddle. That same year he had the honor of being a featured soloist with the Tuscarawas Philharmonic Orchestra.

Calvin Stockdale started his own YouTube channel, "The Stockdale Family," where he posted videos of his growing family, including an annual Christmas video with a different song each year, performed with any extended family that was able to join them.

In the fall of that same year, Charles moved to Temple University to pursue a PhD in organic chemistry. "Kathy and I chatted at the Wilderness Center before Charles began graduate work," said one acquaintance. "She was so proud of his accomplishments (as with each of her boys) and happy to see him move on with his life."

Charles got married in 2015. All three of his brothers were groomsmen and the bridesmaids carried sunflowers. One guest commented that it was the first time they had seen free-spirited Charles wearing shoes.

———

In 2016, Jacob and James released their first CD as the Stockdale Brothers duet, called *Farm Fresh*. "We throw in a lot of stories from the farm and a touch of comedy," James told the Canton Repository. "Jacob will throw in some trick fiddling. One of the fun songs we do is called 'Forty Acres and a Fool.' It's about a farmer whose neighbor moved in from the city and doesn't know much about farming. We do a comedy bit back and forth called 'Arkansas Traveler' between an old farmer who's out in his field and an out-of-towner who is lost comes up asking for directions. Jacob and I also are singing as part of the Straight Tie A Capella Group at the theater this Christmas, and we're throwing in some fiddle and bass and trick guitar work. It's a fun, new experience for us."

When the time came, James went to college to study business at Kent State University Stark and Tuscarawas campuses, studying business management. He planned to pursue a career in the business side of the entertainment world. The tall, handsome lad, with his ready smile, great sense of humor, and outgoing personality, made new friends easily wherever he went. James was a well-known catalyst for family fun. He enjoyed dancing, skiing, farming, fishing, hunting, and camping, displaying an innate love of nature. Not surprisingly, he started dating while at college. He was rumored to be seeing a girl from another bluegrass band, who shared his love of music.

Jacob, on the other hand, had no interest in going to college. His heart lay with farming, and he was happy to stay home and learn all he could about working the land. He grew exotic lettuces and other organic vegetables and raised animals for meat and eggs, selling the excess at markets around the state with his mother. He also gave private lessons in fiddle, mandolin, and guitar in the family home. All he wanted was to be a farmer and a musician and was happiest when playing or teaching music.

James told a reporter, "Our family is no different than

any other. You're always going to have hard times and differences and conflicts. But music was something that kept us together. We always had that in common."

In March 2017, Jacob updated his Facebook profile to a picture of himself holding a magnificent bird of prey. He wrote: "This is my spirit animal. His name is Frank. He brings out my inner falcon."

A friend wrote below the picture, "Please tell me you've become a falconer," to which Jacob responded, "Hum............ Falconer, Fiddler, Farmer. That sounds good."

Tim also took to Facebook to post a *New York Post* article that resonated with him about the effect of too much screen time on children. The article carried the provocative title: "It's Digital Heroin: how screens turn kids into psychotic junkies." Tim added a caption, saying, "So glad we raised our boys low tech. Little fingers and hands are for real life not virtual. I guess that was crazy stuff 9 years ago on our reality TV Wife Swap show Ha."

Also in March, James had his twenty-first birthday and together with Jacob recorded a rendition of "In Tall Buildings," a song by John Hartford that laments growing up, leaving the simple life and having to go to work in the city to earn a living. Before launching into the song, in his casual drawl, James said to the camera, "Thank you everyone for all the birthday well wishes last week. I had a great day full of friends and music. It doesn't get much better than that. You'd think at 21 years old I'd be ready to grow up and join adulthood. Eh, nah ..."

"Not me," Jacob interjected quietly.

"Is there a third option?" James asked rhetorically as Jacob smiled at him. "I wish there was a third option."

7

A BLUEGRASS TRAGEDY

In early June 2017, James and Jacob Stockdale joined family members and friends at the home of their neighbor and long-time family friend, Steve Todd. The Stockdale brothers had a full schedule of concerts, fairs and private parties lined up, but they still enjoyed intimate musical get-togethers with friends and family. However, Jacob left the gathering early because he wasn't feeling well.

A week later, on Thursday, June 15, 2017, the Stockdales' next-door neighbor, Harry McNutt Jr. heard gunshots, not an uncommon thing on the farm. "It was a rapid, you know, boom, boom, boom, boom, boom, boom, then time enough to reload, and another five or six shots so I thought it was target practice," he later told reporters.

Stark County deputies Abatangelo and Leggett arrived at the Stockdale family farm after a 911 hang-up call. As they approached the house, they were greeted by the family dog, which was pacing back and forth from the driveway to the front door, whining. Closing in, they heard a single gunshot coming from inside the house. The deputy immediately jumped off the porch and into the yard, taking cover behind trees and a telephone pole, before running back to the patrol car to retrieve his shotgun. Deputy Leggett took cover behind a vehicle that was in the driveway. The two covered the exits of the house while they waited for backup.

When backup arrived, they approached the house. The young man lying near the front door had apparently suffered a gunshot wound to the head and had a 20-gauge shotgun lying by his side. Guns drawn, still unsure what they were dealing with, the police officers entered the cozy farmhouse. They found another young man lying in the kitchen, blood from a gunshot wound in a pool around him on the floor. The deputies continued their search of the dwelling until they came across a woman upstairs in the bathroom, a gunshot wound to the head.

Even before paramedics arrived, it was clear to the attending officers that the two people inside the house—Kathy and James Stockdale—were dead. The man in the doorway, Jacob Stockdale, was alive. The Bethlehem Fire Service was called and they rushed Jacob to the Cleveland Metro Hospital where he remained in critical condition.

When Tim Stockdale arrived home from work, he was met at the end of the driveway, near the street, by the police officers. They presented Tim, who had escaped the city to avoid gun violence, with news no husband and father should ever have to hear: his wife and one son were dead, and his other son was in critical condition. Then they told him the most shocking thing of all.

They had established that Jacob had made the 911 call and waited for the police to arrive before shooting himself in the head. Twenty-five-year-old fiddle prodigy Jacob, it seemed, had murdered his mother and brother before trying to kill himself.

Tim went to stay with relatives on the night of the murders. Sheriff George T. Maier of the Stark County Sheriff's Department fronted the media to confirm that no prior calls had ever been made to or from the home. There was no criminal past for Jacob Stockdale or any of the family members, and no prior knowledge of mental issues with Jacob or any members of the family.

In response to pressure from reporters, Calvin released a statement: "My family appreciates the prayers and support we are receiving from our friends and the community. We are mourning the loss of my brother and mother and are waiting to learn more about what transpired yesterday afternoon. We thank Sheriff Maier and his staff for their help through this difficult day as well as the staff at Aultman and MetroHealth Medical Center. While support is appreciated, we ask for privacy while our family deals with this tragic loss."

The next day Timothy released his own statement to the press: "Kathy has been my beloved wife of thirty-two years and a wonderful mother to our four sons. She loved nothing more than being a mother and grandmother. She had a strong love of learning and was passionate about her Christian faith, natural health, and organic farming."

Calvin spoke about his brothers: "James, our youngest brother, has always been a catalyst of family fun. Aside from being a gifted musician, James enjoyed dancing and had an innate love of people. James was working on a business degree and hoped to go into the business side of entertainment. He leaves behind many friends and a family that love him dearly. I don't know why Jacob did what he did last week, but I do know he is my brother. I speak for our family when I say we love him and forgive him. The prayers and support for my family have been deeply appreciated and we ask for continued prayers for Jacob's healing—body, mind, and spirit."

It came as no surprise that the remaining Stockdale family chose to forgive and support Jacob. Tim had expressed his belief of loving the sinner, not the sin in the episode of *Wife Swap* when he told the cameras, "I love my children, but I can say to them, 'I love you but I don't love the thing you are doing right now and I want you to stop'."

8

THE SINNER

The Zion Reformed Church in Winesberg, Ohio, the Stockdale family's church, created a memorial fund for the family, and a fund to help with Jacob Stockdale's medical expenses. It raised just under $32,000 from a community that rallied around the family.

Media interest in the tragedy was intense, due in part to the *Wife Swap* connection. Many people judged the family on the half-hour of TV they had seen, which was edited to emphasize the most extreme aspects of the lives of the participants. Those who had watched the show attributed the murder to the strict lifestyle imposed on the boys by their parents. People pointed to the Stockdale's family manual that had been created for *Wife Swap* as an example of Kathy's extreme control over her children, with statements like, "I like things done my way ... I watch over them to make sure it is done right," and her policy of fining the boys 25 cents if they were two minutes late to the breakfast table.

This was further fueled by comments by Laurie Tonkovic after the murders when she spoke to TMZ. "When

I switched the rules, and I was going to let them have fun, and have television and video games and experience life a little bit, [Jacob] ran outside crying. And when I went out after him, I asked what was wrong, and he said that his mom and dad tell him that basically he would burn in hell. He lived in a very controlled environment ... really wasn't allowed to do anything. He worked, he worked, he worked, home-schooled him, wouldn't let him go out amongst society. They're very religious ... They weren't allowed to make choices. I just think that it caught up to them."

Even if *Wife Swap* magnified the rigidity and traditional nature of the Stockdale family home to create contrast and conflict with the Tonkovics, Kathy Stockdale's blog, which included the manuals of both families, suggested that she was not displeased with how her family was presented. Someone in a forum comment observed, "The Stockdales seemed to like the show and there is no evidence that they thought it inaccurate or exaggerated. On the contrary, the blog seems to demonstrate that they were proud to have been featured—and they kept that horrible manual front and central."

However, many who knew the family claimed that the sheltered lifestyle was overblown. They found the family to be open, friendly, and keen to engage with their local community. Several people who took to the comments sections of videos of the episodes expressed surprise, saying that they had known the Stockdale family for many years and knew them only to be loving and supportive.

One family friend said, "The picture of the Stockdale family that their Wife Swap episode paints is really distorted and exaggerated. I'm a lefty atheist so disagree with a lot of the family's beliefs and parenting decisions, but they were a

LOT less strict than Wife Swap depicts, and as human beings, they were actually really sweet people."

Another wrote:

"I knew Kathy personally and she was not the tyrant that everyone is making her out to be. She did micromanage the kids when they were small, but once they became teenagers, those boys did anything they wanted to do. Of course, they didn't WANT to watch TV or things of that sort, but they had internet and cell phones (and were constantly on their phones, in James' case! LOL). James and Jacob were best friends and took road trips together. Skiing trips, hiking/fishing trips. They were very close.

"They were on a strict diet, but even when they were away from home and could "sneak" foods, they didn't because they knew they were trying to better their health. They were on a "leaking gut" diet, and had been introducing new foods right along. James, in particular, had a lot of food allergies.

"I truly don't know what caused this. In my heart, I still feel that Jacob didn't do it. There had to be some other explanation. And if he did, it was a mental or medically induced snap, but not caused by things at home. He LOVED living at home. He was a farmer at heart. He and Kathy raised organic veggies and meats which they sold at various markets. He could have gone to college, and Kathy and Tim encouraged him to do so, but he didn't want to. He learned what he needed by reading and intended on farming and playing music for the rest of his life.

"This family was NOT isolated. They traveled. They were extremely popular and well-liked. The kids were some of the most brilliant minds that I've encountered, very sociable and personable. It is extremely sad to me to see them criticized unjustly."

Their neighbor and friend, Steve Todd, agreed. "They have always been the most admired family, everyone we know loves them and admires them and we have never known anybody that would have said one bad word about any of them. The kids were always great, very loving extremely tight knit family," he told reporters. "They are the most loving, well-adjusted, admirable family you could possibly want to know. It's an absolute shock. It's obviously very tragic."

At the memorial service for Kathy and James Stockdale at the New Pointe Community Church in Dover, the family shared fond and funny memories of James and Kathy. Their favorite hymns, as well as "Troubled Fields" for 54-year-old Kathryn and "The Old Churchyard" for 21-year-old James, played over the auditorium's sound system. They played a video of James singing "Some Day" by Blue Highway, in which the lyrics urge loved ones not to pity the dead but, instead, to prepare to meet them in heaven.

Jacob was still in hospital, but it was clear that his remaining family members were praying just as hard for him as they were for those he had killed.

Jacob remained in hospital in critical condition in the months that followed the shooting. He was not well enough to be charged with anything, though legal experts were sure he would be charged with murder or aggravated murder, and the prosecution could possibly seek the death penalty. Although many of the public felt sure his repressed upbringing was responsible, the sheriff was being more circumspect.

"It's hard to, you know, kind of surmise what the motive may have been," Sheriff Maier said in a press conference. "There's some speculation. Don't really want to get into that part of it. But we will continue to investigate this case and try to determine if there is a motive. [We] just do not know at this time."

By September, the autopsy reports for Kathy and James had been finalized, but the Stark County Coroner's Office could not release them due to the pending investigation. Jacob remained in hospital, his condition unknown to the public. Attempts by law enforcement to interview Jacob did not provide any information, as Jacob had difficulty communicating and his lawyer had recommended he exercise his right to remain silent.

Despite the tragedy, the Stockdale family still made their Christmas video that year. Each of Calvin's four children held on to various instruments once played by the Stockdale Family Band, with 5-year-old Timmy on the fiddle. At the end of the video, they took the opportunity to announce their fifth child was on the way.

For the next year, no new information emerged about Jacob or the shootings, as Jacob continued to be treated for severe head and brain injuries. He was permitted to go and live with a relative in Columbus while receiving outpatient medical treatment at Ohio State University Wexner Medical Center to continue his rehabilitation, as he could not receive adequate care in prison. Prosecutors decided they would wait until Jacob could walk on his own and communicate with them before indicting him.

This finally happened in October 2018, a year and a half after the slayings, when Jacob, now twenty-six, was secretly indicted by a Stark County grand jury on the murder counts. Jacob voluntarily turned himself into the Stark County Jail when he was notified that the indictment had been issued. He pleaded not guilty. It was determined that he would not face the death penalty, but fifteen years to life in prison on each of the murder charges should he be convicted. Jacob's mugshot showed a young man who looked considerably older than the fresh-faced farmer he had been two years before. The gunshot wound had disfigured his face with scars, leaving one eye drooping.

Tim Stockdale gave the press a statement following his indictment, in which he said, "In the past fifteen months our family has begun the healing process. As Jacob has undergone extensive surgeries and physical healing from his wounds, we have all taken the time to try and prepare emotionally for the legal issues ahead. My sons and I continue to love Jacob and we will continue to give our full cooperation to the authorities."

Three months later, in January 2019, Jacob's lawyer entered an official plea of not guilty by reason of insanity in Stark County Court and suggested that Jacob might not be competent to stand trial. At a hearing in May, the court declared Jacob incompetent to stand trial based on a mental health evaluation that his mental illness would prevent him from understanding the charges and assisting in his defense. Jacob was transferred to a secure psychiatric facility, Heartland Behavioral Healthcare Hospital, and his trial was delayed so he could receive mental health treatment. The psychiatrist told the court that it was possible that competency could be restored within a year with intensive treatment and while addressing his depression.

Jacob's remaining family continued to support him while grieving their wife and son, mother and brother.

Charles Stockdale built a rock sculpture in a nearby stream to honor Kathy that Mother's Day.

In October 2019, Jacob's psychiatrist reported that he was able to hold conversations with his music therapist and was able to play intricate compositions during one-on-one interactions, though he either played simpler music or stopped playing altogether when he was in a group therapy setting. Prosecutors suspected that Jacob may have been purposely not cooperating and the court made an order that Jacob's phone records be released so that they could hear how he communicated with his family when he thought nobody was listening.

In November and December 2019, Jacob allegedly twice tried to escape from the psychiatric facility. The first time, staff found him hiding between book stacks in the hospital's library, possibly hoping to find a way to exit the building after the library closed, and the second time he tried blending in with a group of people who were on their way out the door. However, he was easily caught both times and never charged with attempted escape.

That December, Tim and the two older brothers and their families got together for Christmas and, as always, it was music that brought them together. As the children of the ever-growing new generation played with their gifts, Tim, Calvin and Charles sang the catchy, and decidedly unreligious, "Bah Humbug."

Jacob was back in court in February 2020. The psychologist assigned to his treatment team had submitted a report a couple of weeks earlier concluding that Jacob was now deemed competent to stand trial for the murders of his mother and little brother. Jacob remained in hospital and continued to improve, progressing from being disheveled and nonverbal to showering and shaving, participating in group therapy, and taking his medication.

In March 2020, when James should have been turning twenty-four, Tim posted a picture of a tire swing hanging from a tree at sunset. "This. Memories of a time when one little boy just couldn't get enough. James, forever in my heart," he wrote. "I thank God for so many wonderful memories. God in His infinite wisdom knows best. He is the rock on which I lean."

9

CLOSURE DENIED

After many delays, exacerbated by the COVID-19 pandemic, Jacob's trial was finally set for May 2021.

In the lead up to the trial, the court ordered that Jacob be moved from the psychiatric hospital to Stark County Jail as he was deemed an escape risk. A letter from the chief clinical officer at Heartland Behavioral claimed that staff had expressed concerns that, after it was ruled he would not be able to plead insanity at trial, he would try to abscond. They pointed out that he had two documented incidents of attempting to leave the unit in what was believed to be an effort to escape in 2019. They also claimed Jacob had "made statements to the barber that with this new haircut, he resembled his cousin, and if he were able to get keys to the facility, he could walk out."

Heartland staff recommended that "the least restrictive environment for Jacob, while considering the community safety, is the Stark County Jail." The judge, noting that he had to consider whether Jacob was a flight risk while also acknowledging he had a duty to protect the public, moved

Jacob out of the hospital and into Stark County Jail to await trial.

A week before he was due to go to trial, Jacob Stockdale changed his plea to guilty. The judge sentenced Jacob to fifteen years for each murder, the minimum he could have received. However, the sentences were to run consecutively, meaning he would be spending the next thirty years in jail.

The family, who had asked the judge for leniency, declined to speak to reporters about the sentence.

Jacob's guilty plea meant that he avoided a trial, so there was no testimony or evidence that might shed light on his motive for carrying out the crime. When articles and features appeared in the press, public sentiment inevitably leaned toward blaming the strict and restrictive lifestyle shown on Wife Swap for making Jacob "snap" and kill his mother and brother. Commentators were particularly scathing of Kathy, who was depicted as cold and controlling. However, a lot of evidence did not bear this out and her remaining family had only praise and love for her. To those who knew them, the Stockdale family were a close-knit, well-adjusted, and loving family who were always supportive of each other. Calvin and Charles went on to lead successful, independent lives that included visits from their father for family singalongs.

It is not clear if the mental health issues that put Jacob into a secure psychiatric facility for years arose solely from the trauma of the gunshot wound to the head, or whether he had a prior undiagnosed mental illness. According to many studies, in the more fundamentalist religious sects, there is a stigma against mental illness, and the church would rather turn to religion rather than seek psychological help. In deeply fundamentalist societies, participants are encouraged to pray instead of seeking medical assistance for mental health issues, much as they are taught to "pray the gay away" and many conditions are not recognized at all. There is a belief among many evangelical Christians that mental illness can be overcome by Bible study and prayer alone. A combination of a young boy's genuine belief that he and his brother would burn in hell for imagined transgressions and a tendency to psychosis could be a lethal combination.

It is unlikely we will ever know what led Jacob to do the unthinkable that summer day in 2017. However, it is clear that his family will seek solace in their faith. Some time after the murders, Tim posted a Facebook update of a quote by an unknown author:

> *He cried. He knew Lazarus was dead before He got the news. But still, He cried. He knew death here is not forever. He knew eternity and the Kingdom better than anyone else could, yet He wept. Because this world is full of loss and depression and devastation. He wept because knowing the end of the story doesn't mean you can't cry at the sad parts.*

Tim added, "It was 30 months ago today. Because of Christ, I know the outcome in the end. Yes, I still cry at times, but NOT as someone without hope."

THE WIFE SWAP MANUALS

- The Stockdale Family Manual
- The Tonkovic Family Manual

Keep going after the manuals for other books by Eileen Ormsby and a FREE True Crime book

STOCKDALE FAMILY MANUAL

The manual put together by the producers of *Wife Swap* in consultation with the Stockdale Family

---

WELCOME TO OUR HOME!

We're not just a family we're a band - the 'Stockdale Family Band'. We play bluegrass in barn dances and shin-digs all over our area. We have Calvin on banjo, Charles on mandolin, Jacob on fiddle, and James on upright bass. Tim, my husband, is on guitar and I'm the manager. A family that plays together stays together and there's nothing so wholesome as playing old time bluegrass with your favorite people; your family.

We moved to the country to get the boys away from the city. Our children are being raised away from violent language, sexual influences, drinking, smoking, drugs, rap music all the things we left behind in the city. Instead we are raising our children on a diet of wholesome activities and farm work; keeping their minds pure and their bodies healthy and keeping out the influences of modern society. That is why we home-school.

Children need structure, and there's plenty of structure in this house. Our boys know what they are supposed to be doing from sun-up to sun down. They are busy doing chores, running the farm, doing schoolwork and, of course, practicing for performances. Everything they need is here on the farm with their family.

We teach our boys that to succeed you have to have a good work ethic. We raise chickens and process chickens, and what we don't eat we sell. We all pitch in, and I can gut a chicken in under four minutes. The boys receive tokens for every chore they do and an extra token if they do it with a glad heart. They trade their tokens for privileges like listening to the radio or for a stick of gum.

Processed and fast foods are forbidden. Food is nourishment for the mind as well as the body so it's important to eat right. We mostly only eat foods that we grow or we buy from local farmers, that way we know it's healthy and natural. I give my boys a large spoonful of cod-liver oil after dinner to keep their hearts and minds strong.

TV and video games are banned. They produce redundant minds and lazy children. I want my boys to be active, productive and busy every waking moment. Internet access is restricted there's no idle surfing in this house. Instead we enjoy spending time reading to each other, playing music or story-telling.

The boys are not encouraged to date until they are ready to get married. They need to concentrate on building the right foundations for a healthy and moral life NOT thinking about girls. There is plenty of time to worry about that when they have found their bride-to-be and are ready to settle down.

Our motto is: 'it might be a hard life but it's a good life'.

We are the Stockdale Family: Kathy (44), Tim (48), Calvin (19), Charles (16), Jacob (15), James (11) .

HOUSEHOLD

How do you divide the roles?

We live very traditional roles in this household. I stay at home and take care of the cooking, cleaning, teaching our boys and managing the family band. Tim my husband runs the farm with the boys and has a regular full time job delivering animal nutrients to farms across the state. I am completely involved in my children's lives. I stay at home so that I can shape the way they grow up and how they are influenced. It is important for children to have boundaries. They will have to live in a world that has rules and if they don't learn to comply now they're going to have a harder time later in life.

Nothing is free for the boys everything has to be earned. I teach the boys value and respect by using the token system. The boys collect tokens by doing chores with a glad heart to exchange for things that they want. That way they learn to value their privileges and don't come to just expect them.

What are your general views on cleaning?

I have a rule that if you make the mess then you clean it up and as the boys make most of the mess, they do the cleaning. Our family motto is that 'it may be a hard life but it's a good life'.

Do you have a cleaning person or hired help? If so, why? If not, why?

Chores are part of daily life here and a great lesson for the boys to learn from. Hiring someone to clean the house would simply take away that benefit from the boys. Besides no-one said life was easy.

Who does the following, and how often:

Vacuuming & Dusting?

I split the cleaning up and assign rooms to Charles, Jacob and James to vacuum and dust. Making the boys do the work is not only practical but a good exercise for them in learning responsibility.

Cleaning the bathroom?

James is the youngest in the family so he cannot do all the same chores as the older boys. Cleaning the bathroom is something he can achieve and gives him a lesson in responsibility.

Clothes washing & ironing?

I do the washing in the house at least twice a week, we're not into big brand names here, what is practical is what is best.

It is Charles's task to hang the washing up and fold it when it is dry. All the chores in the house need doing, so if one of the boys doesn't like a task then I find something he does like. No one in this family gets a free ride; the boys have to learn that the only way to succeed is by working.

Cleaning the kitchen?

In this house no-one stands around watching everyone

else do work. I teach the boys if you receive then you must give as well. Charles cleans up the dishes after the meals and James cleans the table and helps put the food away.

Other?

We do not look at chores as free slave labor. We are giving our children a good work ethic and a selfless attitude. It keeps us grounded, and bonds us together. We like to teach our boys to work with their hands. This means chores, yard work and cleaning.

PETS

How many pets do you have and what do they require?

We run this farm to provide our family with a sustainable and wholesome life. That means raising our crops and chickens in a free-range, organic environment. Free of steroids and antibiotics. The food that we grow is more natural and tastes better for it.

We have 70 hens, which give us all our eggs, 175 broiler chickens which we process, sell and also use to eat and 1 duck that thinks he is a chicken. Jacob looks after the chicken's everyday; he feeds them in the morning and puts them into their coop in the evening.

COOKING & MEALS

Who cooks for the family?

Food nourishes the mind and the body so it is very important in this family. That's why I insist on giving the boys a spoonful of cod liver oil every dinner time; it helps keep their heart, bones and brain healthy. I spend most of my day cooking three nutritious old fashioned home cooked meals for my family and it is certainly appreciated.

I bring value to home cooked meals by using quality ingredients that either we raised naturally on our farm or that we buy from other local farmers. I treat food with respect by using traditional food preparation, rather than modern methods like microwaves and pasteurizing. It takes me longer to cook but the proof is in the pudding, my food tastes better and is healthier for you and my boys are testament to that. I make sure my boys drink healthily too with my water and dairy kefir. It's a yeast, fruit and water infusion that the boys just love to drink.

We don't eat processed food or anything pre-packaged. It just doesn't have any place in a wholesome nurturing environment. I call all that rubbish 'Franken foods', its science experiments gone wrong. I insist on only eating food that is raised in its natural habitat like our chickens.

Does anyone else ever cook? Who and why?

I like things done my way, the right way. I have started to teach Jacob and Charles how to cook some recipes like sausages and bread but I have to be around to watch over them to make sure they do it right.

Do you all eat together and where do you eat?

The whole family eats together every meal unless Calvin is at college or Tim is out at work and can't get back. It is important family bonding time where we get to talk with one another.

Eating food in our house is a special event and it's a time to be savored so we never rush a meal. Food forms the basis of who we are. Meals are not an obstacle; meals are an event to be shared. Slow food is better than fast food.

What are your top dinners? Please include recipes.

SUNDAY MENU

Dinner Link sausage on bread with sauerkraut and mustard and pickled beets Milk & Water kefir Cod liver oil and butter oil Whole food supplements: Catalyn - everyone 1 each. Digestive enzyme supplement - Mom, Dad, Calvin and James 1 each

MONDAY MENU

Breakfast Giblets (Chicken hearts and gizzards), muesli with cream, sorghum or honey, raisins or dates Dairy kefir or water kefir with flax seed Whole food supplements: Calcium Lactate - James x 6 Whole food supplements: Catalyn - everyone 1 each Digestive enzyme supplements: - Mom, Dad, Calvin and James 1 each

Lunch Fried liver on bread and butter (set out to warm) and mustard Blueberry shakes Whole food supplements: Catalyn - everyone 1 each Digestive enzyme supplement - Mom, Dad, Calvin and James 1 each

Supper Herb baked chicken green salad with fixins, corn on the cob with butter, sliced tomatoes Cod liver oil and butter oil Whole food supplement: Catalyn - everyone 1 each Digestive enzyme supplement- Mom, Dad, Calvin and James 1 each

TUESDAY MENU

Breakfast scrambled eggs, fried rice, hot sauce or salsa Dairy kefir or water kefir with flax seed Whole food supplements: Calcium Lactate James x 6 Whole food supplements: Catalyn - everyone 1 each Digestive enzyme supplement: - Mom, Dad, Calvin and James 1 each

Lunch Sirloin steak, corn on the cob with butter, sauerkraut, greens salad with fixin's. Milk and water kefir Whole food supplements: Catalyn - everyone 1 each, Digestive enzyme supplement: - Mom, Dad, Calvin and James 1 each

Supper Sardines on hot buttered toast with mustard, sauerkraut, tomato soup, pickled eggs. Milk and water kefir Whole food supplements: Catalyn - everyone 1 each Digestive enzyme supplements - Mom, Dad, Calvin and James 1 each

Do you or anyone in the family have any special dietary requirements? Is there anything you won't eat?

I don't let the boys eat snacks, cookies, candy and especially not fizzy sodas. These are all nutritionally bad for you. If the boys come home with candy that someone has given them then I buy it off them and then throw it away. James has intolerance to dairy.

How often do you eat out at restaurants? Do you take the kids?

We never eat out at restaurants its just not something we like to do. We eat better food at home and it costs less.

What kind of restaurants do you go to?

Even when we're on the road we take our own fast food with us. Apples, cold chicken, crackers and cheese. We can usually survive on this until we get back home from a trip.

How often do you or your family eat fast/junk food? What kind do you eat?

Processed pre-packaged food is a gross resemblance of the real thing. It is not real food for real people. We never eat fast food. In fact any time James has eaten it, he has thrown up. We try to eliminate all processed food, because it is unnatural and un-healthy for you.

SHOPPING

Who does the grocery shopping?

Living on a farm means we grow most of our own food so we don't use the store too often. When we do we try and shop locally. That way we are putting dollars back in to the community. We buy what we can't grow ourselves, which is bananas, rice, canned meats and fish, Salmon and herring and a few spices.

How often?

During summer I go to the store once a month but always combine it with a trip for the boys like taking Jacob to his fiddle class, that way we can save on fuel bills.

Does anyone help with the grocery shopping?

I buy all the supplies myself. Sometimes the boys come with me but I usually go on my own.

Who chooses what is bought?

I am the cook for this family so I choose what is bought. I pay extra special attention to how food is grown and where it comes from that way I can be sure it is healthy.

WEEKDAY MORNING ROUTINE

What time do you get up?

It is important for the boys to start the day with a hot wholesome hearty meal so I get up before them to prepare their breakfast. I wake up at 7am and go down to the kitchen to start cooking. It takes a little extra time to make but giving the boys the right food means they can last without snacking until lunch.

What time does everyone else get out of bed?

Tim gets up at 5:30am in the morning to go to work. I always prepare breakfast for him the night before so he can heat it up in the morning and have a cooked breakfast before he leaves the house.

Now that Calvin is working outside of the home, he no longer has as many chores or tasks to do and I leave him to manage his own time, but he still makes it for breakfast in the morning with the rest of the family. Calvin usually leaves for work at 9:30am.

I wake the boys up at 7:30am. When breakfast is nearly ready I call James, Jacob and Charles to the table and tell them that they have four minutes before breakfast starts. I make sure to set the oven timer so that I know when their time is up. If they don't come down to breakfast on time I give them two minutes to arrive and charge them 25 cents for being late. If they continue being late I increase the charge every two minutes until they come to the table.

It is good to teach children to be on time and the financial penalty seems to really work. All the money they pay in fines goes into the jar on the windowsill. Charles has the most amount of fines to pay, he never gets out of bed on time.

Are you 'morning people?'

If the boys are playing music in the evening it's hard to stop them so we end up going to bed a little later around 11pm. If we go to bed late then we always sleep in to maybe 8am the next morning.

What is the morning routine in your house?

I have breakfast with the boys at 8am. Feeding the boys a good hot hearty meal in the morning means that they can last until lunchtime without snacking. If the boys don't finish a meal then they can't eat anything until then next meal so they always finish what's on their plate.

After breakfast Charles and James clean up the breakfast dishes, while Jacob goes out to feed the chickens and put any things that need recycling into the special bin.

Who prepares breakfast? Does the family eat it together?

I always prepare breakfast. Even if Tim is rushing off very early in the morning to one of his jobs I prepare his breakfast the night before so that he can start the day with a healthy hot breakfast.

What time do the kids leave for school?

I homeschool James, Jacob and Charles, which starts first thing after, breakfast and chores. I have a rule that they are not allowed to do anything else until their schoolwork is done unless it is music, which is part of their education.

Homeschooling the boys means that they are not affected by outside influences and are able to grow up in a safe and wholesome environment.

Do you ever get to sleep in?

We do not live by the clock. We live according to farm seasons and seasons of family life. Our schedule responds to the families needs. We sometimes stay up late at night till 11pm to make time for the boys and their dad to practice. When this happens we all sleep in.

DAYTIME

What is your schedule for the day?

I run this house with structure and schedules. The boys

all have chores and tasks to accomplish after breakfast and I make sure that they do them. James scrubs the bathroom, Charles folds and hangs up the laundry and all three of them have to make their bed. I check up on each chore to make sure it is done correctly, my boys are so well trained that they usually do them to standard but I have detailed reminders of what is expected in each room in case they forget.

While the boys are doing their morning chores I put together their daily schedule sheets listing everything I want them to accomplish.

Charles Math Science Mandolin and guitar practice Gather trash at house and take all trash cans to the road for pickup Weed whip Mowing Garden weeding and rototilling

Jacob Math Science History Memorization Drafting fiddle, Chick brooder @ 4 times/day including before breakfast and at the end of the day, Clean nest boxes Clean House clutter Garden weeding and rototilling

James Reading Math Logic Memorization Drafting Suzuki, Fiddle Clean bath and sink Clean kitchen sink Get the mail Sweep porch, clean steps clutter Water garden

I always start home school at 10am with a ring of the bell outside. By teaching the boys myself I have control over what is taught and what morals to impart. I don't believe in leaving something as important as education decisions to anybody else. Home schooling the boys preserves our way of life and ensures that the boys grow up in a wholesome environment. Multi-tasking is essential in this house. While the boys are schooling I keep one eye on them and start to make my nutritious water kefir or sauerkraut. Or work on organizing the bands arrangements in my office.

Chores and a good work ethic are the foundations of this family. Most other children don't know how to mow a lawn or weed whack, my boys do and they are learning the true benefit of a good days work. After an hour of home schooling I send the boys out to start on their outside chores. Jacob lets the chickens out, feeds them and picks up their eggs. And then goes to help Charles mowing one of the fields.

Charles is also responsible for weed whipping. James waters the front garden and then sweeps the porch. There are always maintenance works and farm tasks to be done around here so the boys help along with Tim when he is home. If the boys do a chore or task then I reward them with a token on the board. It is important to reward good behavior that way they learn not only from the benefit but through positive reinforcement. The boys can trade in tokens for privileges later in the day.

I start working on lunch at around 12noon and like to serve lunch for everyone at 1pm. Food is important nourishment in my family and not just for the body but for the mind too. A healthy body and healthy mind that's what we strive for here. The boys always clean up after lunch, Charles loads the dishwasher and James and Jacob help clear the table and empty the plates.

After lunch the boys get together and practice their music. Some music these days can only be classed as a bad influence, but not the Bluegrass the boys play. At 4pm the boys have their debate lesson. Teaching the boys to communicate and think through an argument is a vital part of their education. It is also a good way for them to meet and to learn to socialize with other young people.

If it is chicken processing day then we usually start around 3pm and spend the rest of the afternoon processing the chickens for sale. It can be slightly messy, eviscerating a chicken but that is part of farm life.

If the boys have a performance in the evening then I like to prepare a light hot meal for them around 5pm before getting them ready for their performance. I get the boys to load the CDs I sell at the concerts into the car and make sure they have all of their music and equipment loaded.

When we are not having a performance then I would start preparing dinner at 5pm. We always have a sit down family dinner and eat together at 6pm. It so important to take time over your meal and really enjoy spending time together.

What time do the kids finish school and how do they get home?

Schoolwork and music have priority in this house so the boys must do their schoolwork first before attending to any of the outside chores.

Do they have any extra classes or activities after school? Who takes them and picks them up?

We do not push the boys to play sports because of the competitive nature of team games. The glory seeking can encourage too much of a self centered aspect that is not desirable in clean living children.

The boys pay for all the extra activities that they do with money that they earn themselves. It is a valuable lesson for them to learn that nothing is free in this world and if you want to do something then you have to pay for it yourself.

Raising the boys in a wholesome environment means teaching them activities that will be useful to them in the future. I think it is good for them to learn to be practical with their hands so Jacob and Charles have woodworking class on Mondays from 6:15 and all three of the younger boys have scouts on a Tuesday evening at 7pm.

Charles has Mandolin lessons on Thursday at 2pm and Jacob has fiddle lessons at 4pm.

When do the kids do their homework? Do you or your partner help them?

Teaching a child that it is ok to fail is not acceptable in my book. I never pass the boys if they have a C or even a B they have to achieve an A grade in a subject before moving on. That way they are working towards mastering the subject.

EVENING

If you work outside the home, what time do you get home from work?

My life is centered on the home and the boys. I am the mother, school teacher, cook and band manager in this family. I get the boys up and schedule their day from the moment they wake up to the moment they go to sleep. I don't believe in having idle hands or idle boys so I try to keep them busy and teach them a good work ethic. I provide a safe wholesome environment for the boys to grow up in and I monitor and control the inputs into their life so that they receive the right education.

I do not allow the boys to watch TV at all and if they want to trade in their tokens to watch a movie or listen to the radio then it is from a selection that I have pre-vetted. I don't want them listening to or watching horror movies or inappropriate language. It is important to limit the contact the boys have with the ills of the world. Just because it exist doesn't mean it is good or healthy and especially not for children.

What time is dinner? Who cooks it?

I spend most of my afternoon preparing the dinner for the family. Our family's schedule revolves around our meal times. I serve dinner at 6pm usually depending on what time Tim is back from work.

What is your dinner routine?

The boys set the table and prepare the salad for dinner. We nourish our minds as well as our bodies with wholesome home cooked food that I prepare. To keep the boys healthy I make them eat a spoonful of cod liver oil at every dinnertime. The main dinner is the most important meal of the day, we gather round our kitchen table and praise God for the food that we receive before eating.

Who cleans up after dinner?

The boys clean up after dinner so that they learn that to receive they must also give Charles is responsible for putting the plates in the dish washer and James help clear the table.

What happens after dinner?

After dinner the boys start practicing their music. I make sure there is regular practice sessions scheduled into their day and even put up lyrics in the bathroom so that they never miss an opportunity to learn them. Music is one of the ways we bond together as a family and is a good life skill that they can use at any age. We have a band contract to outline everyone's responsibilities and the need to turn up to practices on time. If the boys don't know what is expected of them then they can't be held accountable when they do something wrong. The boys are very keen musicians so it can get pretty loud in the house but it is better than everyone going off to sit in their rooms on their own.

Are your kids allowed out during the week? If so do they have a curfew?

We spend most of our time together as a family and do not really go out late at night. In the city, families are constantly distracted from being together. It's too difficult to compete with all the modern entertainment and activities available. I see the farm setting as being a much more natural way for a family to be a family. It is easier to control and censor the inputs into the children's lives being out here in the countryside.

Do your kids have set bedtimes?

I run this family to a tight ship with their schedules but we are not slaves to the clock. If the boys have been performing in their Bluegrass band or have been practicing then they stay up a little later. Usually James and Jacob go to bed at 9:30pm and Charles goes to bed at 10.00pm. Calvin decides when he goes to bed. Once in bed they usually read for a while before lights out. If we are to bed late we can always get up a little later in the morning and adjust our schedules for the day.

What is the bedtime routine with the kids?

We find it very difficult to stop what we are doing in the evenings, especially if the boys have started playing music they become so involved. If they are not playing music, I will read to the boys from one of the 'classics'. After all, if you read well you will think well.

What else do you do in the evening before you go to bed?

After the boys have gone to bed Tim and I spend time with each other talking through the days events and planning the days ahead. With so much going on all the time it is important to us to have time with one another.

What time do you go to bed?

I will go to be bed at around 11:00pm after the boys have gone to bed.

WEEKENDS

What does the family do on Saturday?

The weekend is where we all come together as a family. Tim always has a project on the farm to do and includes the boys in helping him, whether it's chopping firewood, maintenance or setting up the electric fence to ward off groundhogs. I usually spend the day catching up on house cleaning and organizing any extra band activities.

Living on the farm gives us a simple life. Unlike living in the city we do not need lots of material possessions out here.

What's your Sunday morning routine?

We always have breakfast together on Sunday mornings before going to church at 10am. We get back from church at 12:30 and eat a small lunch at 1:30pm.

What's your Sunday afternoon routine?

We have our main dinner in the evening on Sundays as a family so usually we eat just a light meal during the day. After lunch I let the boys leave clearing up till later as they are always rushing off to help Tim with some project or picking up a fiddle or banjo to play. If we move one of the cars into the driveway we can pick up a local Bluegrass radio show so we usually spend the afternoon on the porch listening to that.

What do you do Sunday evening?

I start preparing dinner around 4.30pm on Sundays. I usually take an hour to get everything just right and prepared and we like to eat by 6.30pm. Before we eat, the boys sing a prayer thanking the Lord for the food we receive.

After dinner the boys clean up and we spend the evening conversing with one another or listening to the boys play music. I often read the boys a story from one of the classics before they go to bed.

EDUCATION

How do you feel about education?

My aim is to give the boys the ability to explore the world in a safe environment. There is no playground bullying or peer pressure here and I do not allow criticism between the boys.

No-one fails my classes. They are only allowed to continue on with a subject when they have mastered it. So they all get A's.

It is important that the boys are well read and that they can speak properly. Higher education is not so important though as it doesn't always equate to success. We teach the boys they can be successful through entrepreneurial self employment by making them earn their own money. There is no 'free' money on this farm!

Did you or your partner go to college?

Both Tim and I went to college and studied 'agriculture'. That's where we met each other in agronomy club and started to date before getting married.

Although I dated when I was at college I don't want my boys to date until they are ready to get married. Charles is already asking questions about it so I sit down with him and explain that it is not the best thing to do just yet. Teenagers can suffer emotional traumas or even diseases by focusing their lives on dating too early. I remember wasting so much of my time on dating that now that I look back it just seems so pointless. When they have established themselves then they can go out looking but not until then.

Do you home school your children?

I home school the boys to keep the family unit together and to be able to limit the influence of the outside world on our children's lives so we can create the type of childhood that is most healthy for them.

Since we have farm and music demands all through the year we keep up with book learning by studying year round. It also helps the boys not to forget over the summer what they learned.

Are there any rules about homework?

All schoolwork is homework. I help the boys and then the older boys help the younger brothers. Delegation is vital to our home life and school and its never too early or late to learn that we need each other to succeed in life.

Is it important that your children go to college?

The boys don't get anything free from us and money doesn't grow on trees around here, they have to work for their own money. Even though Calvin has started at college I don't think that it is always a recipe for success. We believe in entrepreneurship first and foremost.

LEISURE AND SOCIAL LIFE

What do you do as a family?

Life is not about entertainment and fun. I do not promote a lot of leisure time for the boys. A lot of emphasis in the teen world is placed on hanging out with friends. We do not hang out. I insist that the boys have a focus and purpose to any activity so that the boys do not become corrupted by meaningless relationships.

What do you do as a couple?

We nurture a family environment so we are together all the time, as it should be. If we do have time to ourselves then we spend it lying in the fields looking at the sky or stars or just enjoying one another's company outside on the porch.

Do your kids have their own social life outside of the family?

The boys don't hang out at malls. If they socialize it is through useful and wholesome activities like debate class where they learn life long communication skills in a fun environment. The boys have made some good friends though debate class with other home schooled children and occasionally get together here at our home to discuss speech and debate topics with one another.

How much of a role do friends play in your life?

My family is the cornerstone of my life. I teach the boys that you need to work together to achieve anything in this world.

KIDS

What kind of parent are you?

It is important to be a parent first and foremost when

you have children. Children are not independent people and need to be directed and guided through life. We create a safe nurturing environment for the boys to grow up in.

Do you parent like you were parented?

I am definitely stricter with my boys than my parents were on me but America is a very different country now than when I was growing up.

I try to limit the amount of influence the 21st century has on my boys so that they can grow up in a wholesome and carefree manner. Video games, TV and dating are all banned in this house. I want my boys to concentrate on the good things in life like family unity, music and education.

Not allowing my boys to watch television and play video games is one of the sole reasons they are who they are today. I am always asked how I get the boys to be so interested in playing instruments, it's more like how do I stop them from playing all the time. Their daily lives are not distracted with modern technological obstacles that entertain them to death. I always say if it's fun it doesn't mean you have to do it.

Do you and your partner disagree about parenting?

I am the disciplinarian in the house but Tim backs me up. We both believe in home schooling because we want to preserve our lifestyle, our family unity, and our morals. With home schooling we are able to control the impurities that come into their lives and give the boys a great education.

Are your children well behaved?

We try to have not only wholesome foods but also wholesome attitudes and wholesome speech so we do not swear in our household. My boys are very well behaved just like we have raised them.

By fining the boys financially and by taking away their privileges the boys have learned what is expected of them. I use the token system to reward them not only for behavior but for attitude as well.

Charles is the independent thinker of the four boys and is always questioning why we do the things we do. I am sure he would rather be out playing sports all the time. We have even had to stop him from climbing the roof of the house.

What are your hopes and dreams for your children?

I don't want my boys to make the same mistakes that I made, like spending too much time on dating so I try to instill the lessons that I learned as I grew up. That way they can benefit from my experiences.

What are your feelings about chores?

There are no free rides in this house. Chores are a mandatory part of living in this family and it teaches the boys a good work ethic and team spirit.

Do you have house rules?

The first rule of this house is to obey your parents. Teaching the boys respect is vital in this modern world where so many children disrespect adults. We don't tolerate any of the boys hurting each other physically or verbally and insist that if they make a mess they clean it up.

There is no free roaming of the internet. You have to have a purpose and a destination to go to and then you're done. The children are at a critical age when it is necessary to protect their innocence.

Do you discipline your children? How often and for what?

We use the token chart system to install discipline. For every chore or task that the boys have to do they receive a token for completing it and another token for doing it on time or with a good attitude. If they don't complete the task or have bad attitude they have a token taken away. The boys can then redeem privileges for tokens, like listening to a radio program.

How often do you and your children talk?

By limiting and controlling media and other modern distractions in the house we spend more time together as a family doing the simple things in life like talking and playing music together.

How much time do you spend without your children?

Our family lives, works, learns, eats and plays together. The whole point of our way of life is to create a nurturing family environment for our children. My boys are learning a great lesson on how to interact with elders. When Calvin or Tim come home everyone gathers together and listens to them tell stories of their day.

THE RELATIONSHIP

How would you describe your relationship with your partner?

We both look out for each other. We are a partnership raising our children in a safe and controlled environment for their benefit.

What is the best thing about your relationship?

We need very little external material things to make our

relationship happy. We enjoy the simple things in life and we enjoy them together.

What annoys you about your partner?

Tim finds it hard managing his own time. He lives very much in the present and doesn't think about the consequences of spending 100% of his own time on the here and now without planning for the future.

What do your partner and you disagree about the most?

Tim and I are pretty unified in our thinking because we spend the time to talk through our thoughts with one another and with the family.

But we do disagree on whether to stay on a farm of this size. The farm is not paying for itself and Tim is taking extra work outside which means he is spending even more time away from the family. Tim wants to try to keep the farm because he likes the lifestyle but it must become sustainable.

What happens when you disagree?

We don't disagree very often but when we do we talk out our problems with each other. If one of us feels more strongly then the other defers.

Do you disagree in front of the children?

I'm too verbal to be quiet; if I disagree then I say what I think.

FINANCES

Are you spenders or savers?

Running a farm is definitely an expensive business. Tim has taken extra work which has taken him away from the farm and the family but the extra money is useful and needed. You can't always grow everything but we try to be as self sufficient as possible. We are definitely savers and teach the boys that if they want something then they have to work for it just like in the real world, no-one is going to give it to you for free.

Who controls the money?

I am very thrifty in saving money and we share all financial decisions.

How much allowance do the children receive per week? Do they have to earn their allowance?

The boys don't receive any money allowance. You don't get that when you're older so they should learn that now. We teach the boys to be entrepreneurial in earning money for themselves. They sell chickens that we raise and work on other farms during the summer. The boys must pay for all their own music lessons and debating classes just like the real world.

How much do you spend on food & household items per week?

We grow most of our food ourselves and try to live as sustainable as possible. When we have to buy food and household items we try to buy locally from other farmers. We spend about $30 a week on household items.

How much do you each spend on treats or vices per week?

We don't spend anything on treats and vices; it doesn't cost anything being together as a family spending time with each other.

ANYTHING ELSE YOU WANT TO TELL ABOUT YOUR HOUSEHOLD?

We are raising our family on a homestead, where we live simply and grow our own food. We have found the combination of farm work, books and music combined with wholesome food and a nurturing family environment to be a great foundation to raise children. This life is definitely not the easiest but it is certainly the most rewarding.

TONKOVIC FAMILY MANUAL

The manual put together by the producers of *Wife Swap* in consultation with the Tonkovic Family

WELCOME TO OUR HOME!

Everybody knows when the Tonkovics are throwing a party we can have 150 kids out here; dancing, laughing, hooking up, fooling around together. We're famous for our parties; even the sheriff drops by sometimes to make sure no-one is drinking and driving. We would never let that happen we have an open door policy so if you've had a drink you're welcome to crash out in the basement along with everybody else.

I'm called "Mama T" by my children's friends, and my husband is known as "El Supremo". Together we are the heads of the Tonkovic clan. Our kids' friends come and go as they please in our home. I don't like it when it's quiet. When I hear people talk and laugh I know they're having fun. It's important for me to know that people are happy. That's why we make sure we provide a home that people feel comfortable being themselves in. When my guests are happy, I'm happy. Being around kids keep us young!

Our son Paul is a rapper known as T-VIC. He raps about sex, violence, current affairs, whatever he's feeling at the time! He's really creative, but his raps can be a bit graphic and his language is terrible but that's rap I guess. He's pretty serious about his rap and he's so good at it, I can't imagine that he won't succeed. Mama T and El Supremo are behind him all the way.

Our daughter Meghan is a real beauty. She's been modelling for 2 years. She's modelled clothes in magazines and swim suits on the internet. She's trying to move into video. She's already been featured as a dancer in a local music video so we've all got really high hopes for her success. Me and her father are extremely proud of what she's achieved so far.

We feel that education is a wonderful thing, but it's important for our kids to know that they can't learn everything from a book! Life skills and common sense can take you farther than anything you learn in school. If they slip up with their grades it's ok because we know that good grades do not equal good character!

Our kids' partners also live with us. Hector is Meghan's boyfriend he sleeps in the basement, because Meghan is only 17. I am very open with her about sex and contraception but Hector still sleeps downstairs as a mark of respect to me and El Supremo. Because they are a little bit older Paul and his girlfriend Samantha share a bedroom. As El Supremo says " I'd rather it happen under our roof than somewhere on the street!"

The kids get an easy ride here. They don't listen to us, so we've given up trying to get them to do anything round the house. Chores are for little kids anyway. The kids know that if they want money for anything all they have to do is just ask. I control the purse strings in our house. None of the kids have jobs, except for Paul, but who knows how long that will last! If anyone, including my husband John, needs money for cigarettes, gas for the car, or a few bucks for snacks, they know to come to me.

The family spends a lot of time fishing because it's a fun activity that everyone enjoys and the lake is right across the street! If the kids aren't hanging out in the house you can find them nearby, fishing and just hanging out! The kids are into fishing so much that they have stayed out until 5 in the morning just waiting for a big catch!

We think it's very important for children to be able to express themselves. I don't want to raise children that are sheltered and have no concept of what the real world is like! We think that children should be given the freedom to make mistakes. We believe that, "You must let your children fall in order to stand tall"!

We are the TONKOVIC's. Laurie (45), John (52), Paul (20), Meghan (17), Hector Sivero(19), and Samantha Nyman(20).

KIDS

What kind of parent are you?

We're laid back parents. I believe life experiences are the most important thing to shape children. If I sheltered my kids and kept them from the world I would be doing them a disservice. I think that a parent who micromanages every-thing their kids do and shelters them is awful because the kids aren't prepared for real life.

Do you parent like you were parented?

I think we both got the basic tools on how to raise children from our parents. But we definitely don't parent the way we were parented. Our home is much more open. It's okay to make mistakes here. My kids tell me things I could never tell my parents. John was a hellraiser and a heart-breaker growing up. He never thought he'd see 21, so there isn't anything the kids could tell him that he would find shocking. The kids know they have nothing to hide from us, because chances are we've experienced the same thing already.

Do you and your partner disagree about parenting?

We disagree on punishments, and how little we really do punish the kids. For instance, when Paul gets a speeding ticket John will want to take away the car. But I don't see the point in doing that. The kid already got the speeding ticket. His punishment is finding a way to pay the fine.

Are your children well behaved?

The worst thing you can say about them is that they are always cussing around here and not lifting a finger to pick up anything and even though I spend a lot of time screaming at them to clean up their language or the house, nothing seems to work. I would like a little more help around the house from the kids, but I don't know how to make that happen.

What are your hopes and dreams for your children?

I think my children have what it takes to follow their dreams. Rap music is Paul's life. He has the skills and talent. He can pick up an instrument and make it happen. I help him out by buying his microphone, the producing equip-ment, the keyboard, and his guitar. It's important for me to know that he is happy and feels supported.

His lyrics are graphic, I know. Paul will be the first one to tell you that his music is vulgar and explicit. . I hear the same if not worse from other rappers out there. His lyrics are part of the music, not him. When I see him perform and see the way crowds react to him at open-mic nights, I know he's doing the right thing.

Meghan is a model, but I don't know if she wants to do it forever. She loves kids and talks about owning a day care or being a pre-school teacher. But as a model, she's a born natural. She loves it and she's so good at it. She also has dreams of being an actress but has trouble reading and memorizing her script.

The most important thing for my children is to be happy and to be okay with how they end up as adults. They don't have to be super successful in their careers, but if they enjoy life and are proud of who they are, then I've done my job.

What are your feelings about chores?

We don't have chores in this house! It's not worth the time and aggravation we spend fighting with our kids to get things done, so we just do it ourselves and get it over with. Eventually things get done, and they are rarely done by anyone but me!

Do you have house rules?

The closest things we have to house rules are for the kids to make sure none of their friends' park in the driveway and that we have no tolerance for drinking and driving.

Do you discipline your children? How often and for what?

We don't discipline our children because they don't listen to anything we say and grounding doesn't work because they're too old. We tried to ground Meghan once and she just laughed at us and said, "I'm not in fifth grade anymore." I didn't find that amusing, but I'm terrible at sticking to any punishments I make for the children.

How often do you and your children talk?

When do we not talk? We talk all the time about everything and anything and I mean anything.

How much time do you spend without your children?

We barely spend anytime away from our children because they are such a huge part of our lives. The only time spent away from the children is when John and I are at work.

COOKING & MEALS

Who cooks for the family?

If you're hungry, eat! Nobody cooks for the family in a formal way. We all decide on what we are going to eat and we get to it. Everyone here is old enough to feed themselves so they don't need to ask for my permission. If we decide we want to grill some burgers or steaks - Hector and Dad are doing it because they like to grill. Paul is great with breakfast like cheesy eggs and pancakes. Other than that, you can find us eating any type of junk food from sugared cereal to ice cream to fill us up. Our kitchen is open 24/7!

Does anyone else ever cook? Who and why?

There are always snacks being made, and numerous people coming in and out of the house eating them. We have a very help yourself mentality when it comes to eating around here.

Do you all eat together and where do you eat?

We eat all over the house. Even if we are eating at the same time, we are never all in the same place. You can always find John eating on the couch in front of the TV and the kids eat a lot of food in their rooms. You can find plates of half eaten food and cans of soda all over this house!

What are your top three dinners? Please include recipes.

What dinners? We don't cook entire dinners. We're a family of people who snack all the time. Some of our favorites are:

1) Guacamole

8 avocados 1 large onion 1 large tomato

Peel the Avocado's and take the pits out, chop up the onion, and the tomato and put it all in a bowl. Add a little lemon juice and salt. Stir up until creamy and serve.

2) Vegetable Salad

1 head of cauliflower 1 package of broccoli 1 package of mild cheddar cheese 1 package of mozzarella cheese 1 bottle of Ranch Dressing 1 large Vidalia onion

Chop everything up and add the cheese. Add the dressing you might not need a whole bottle of dressing, you need to taste it and see how much is needed. Stick your hands in the bowl to mix the ingredients.

3) Burger Nights!

We love to go through the drive thru to get fast food burgers. One night a week, so we get them by the bagful and bring them back to the house.

How often do you eat out at restaurants? Do you take the kids?

We eat out with the kids at restaurants once a week, but there is no limit to how much take out food this family consumes. We're no strangers to drive-thrus and we have pizza delivered to the house a few times a week.

What kind of restaurants do you go to?

We go out for Italian a lot and we have a Japanese Steak House that we love to go to for special occasions.

We love to try something different and eat a variety of foods, because we are a family that loves to eat. Everything goes here, from Mexican food to practically any other type of ethnic food you can imagine. It's kind of like a smorgasbord!

How often do you or your family eat fast/junk food? What kind do you eat?

Junk food is all we really eat around here. We never run out of chips, dips, snacks, and soda pop. We are always stopping for burgers at drive-thru's whenever we get hungry! It's quick and much easier than trying to cook a meal at home that's going to please everybody. Too many people worry about dying from fast food, but you know what, you're going to die of something!

EDUCATION

How do you feel about education?

There's a lot more knowledge you can gain from the street than out of a book. Education is important, but there are many ways to get one that have nothing to do with reading books or getting good grades. Some people are meant to go to school and some aren't. You can read every book in the world, and not know a damn thing about what's going on next door!

I don't think it's important for kids to get straight A's because I know my kids are trying as hard as they can. They can bring home their D's on their report card, but I know they've given their all. I can't ask for more than that.

Did you or your partner go to college?

I did go to college but I never graduated. I ended up getting a certification. John and I got our education through on the job training and classes. We both feel that books can only take a person so far.

Do you home school your children?

We don't homeschool because it doesn't teach kids about life, it isolates them. Kids need to be around people. It's really important that kids go to high school and learn to be social around peers their own age, and experience the high school years for themselves. Part of getting an education is learning about life, the "drama" of being a teenager, and meeting new people. When you're home schooling, you're staying in a house doing nothing and I don't think that's good for kids at all.

What schools can provide, you can't get at home. The kids you meet in school can be the friends you have for life. When you home school your children, you are only allowing your kids to be exposed to your opinions, to your experiences and you aren't allowing your child to develop on their own. I believe it's important for kids to express themselves and they can't do that properly when they are being held back from the world in a sheltered environment.

Are there any rules about homework?

We've never had any rules about homework because we think it's the children's responsibility to get their work done on their own.

Is it important that your children go to college?

I'd like the kids to go to college but I know it's not for everyone. For John and I school it was social hour. John was a swimmer and had no time for homework. I just conned my teachers to get by and they ended up loving me! We never graduated with our classes, but we got our GED's and made out great. Finding a trade and working with your hands is a fine living and nothing to be ashamed of because some of the best jobs aren't found in an office.

LEISURE AND SOCIAL LIFE

What do you do as a family?

We don't have "scheduled" family time, but we try to do a lot together as a family. We love playing cards, especially poker. We have a 5 buck buy in to play, but if the kids aren't working and don't have the money we chip in. The only catch is, if the kids win, we don't see a penny of that money. If we're lucky we might get our five dollars back.

What do you do as a couple?

We don't do much as a couple. Maybe we go to an occasional work party together or something but we never have date nights. At the last holiday work party of mine that we went to, John got so trashed that I had to hold him up to keep him from falling over. I don't think we'll go back next year.

Do your kids have their own social life outside of the family?

If we're not having a party here, the kids go over to friends' homes to attend parties. I know all the kids that my children hang out with. I don't like them all, but I don't believe it's my job to pick and choose my children's friends. The kids will hang out with bad elements more if I protest, so I let them learn on their own from their decisions. They usually see that I was right in the end. You have to let them learn from their own mistakes.

How much of a role do friends play in your life?

Friends play a huge role in our life. I consider my children's friends to be our friends as well. It's all about the open door policy that John and I have here in the house. It comes from love. We want to create a place where kids are free to be whomever they want. We have brought so many of our children's friends into this family because we want to provide them with a loving home. I enjoy being around the kids, and want them to feel that this a safe place for them to be whomever they want without judgement or consequence. The kids keep us young and we thrive just being around them!

This is definitely a party house! We've had parties here with 150 people in the house and yard. We always know what's going on here. We would rather it all happen under our roof instead of somewhere out in the street where people don't have their best interests at heart.

HOUSEHOLD

What are your general views on cleaning?

I hate to clean because it's no fun and it takes away from time that could be spent just enjoying life. There has to be a health hazard happening for me to really buckle down and do it!

Cleaning isn't that important to us. It's not unusual to see 10 or 12 empty soda cans on a table just waiting to be picked up. The philosophy is, "We'll get to it when we get to it." When John starts to see the kids' fingerprints on the light switches, then he'll spring into action and lend a hand when it comes to cleaning.

How do you divide the roles?

In this house, I am responsible for the day to day mini-cleanups and my husband John is the main provider.

The kids are great at making a mess in the house, and not much else! The most you will see is Hector offering to cut the grass every two weeks or so. Paul is supposed to take out the garbage but it never happens. I would get on the kids more for not taking a part in cleaning up, but I get tried of yelling at them. It's just easier if I do it myself.

Do you have a cleaning person or hired help?

We used to have a cleaning person a couple of years ago and it was great. Eventually, she became lazy and started to slack off, because she started to get to know us and felt she could take advantage of us because we are nice people. It became a waste of money! We decided we didn't need a cleaning person after all and it's not like we live in Beverly Hills where having a maid is a regular thing.

Who does the following, and how often:

Vacuuming & Dusting?

My husband and I vacuum 2 times a week downstairs.

We never touch the upstairs because it takes too long and we consider the upstairs to be the kids space.

We've tried to clean the upstairs before, but as soon as we finish, the kids make sure to mess it up again. What's the point in wasting our time cleaning up after them? If they want to live that way it's their prerogative!

Cleaning the bathroom?

We try to clean the downstairs bathrooms once a week. John hates cleaning out toilet bowls, so he compromises by straightening the towels and I go back and finish the rest.

The kids' bathrooms upstairs are disaster areas! If you have to use their bathrooms, I suggest two things: 1) Watch your step because the floor is covered in dirty clothes and wet towels and 2) Check for toilet paper before you go to the bathroom.

The kids are so inconsiderate when it comes to changing toilet paper rolls when they start to run low. If there is one piece of toilet paper left on the roll, in their minds, there's enough there for the next person to use!

Clothes washing & ironing?

I hate to do laundry, because it takes up too much time, so the laundry is not done very often. I tell the kids that if they don't feel like washing, they are welcome to start digging through the pile of clothes in their rooms and on the washing room floor! They're bound to find something in those piles of clothes that they can wear again.

Air freshener goes a long way in this house because it covers up the smell of our clothes in between washes. We don't iron because most of our clothes don't need it, and if they do need ironing, we avoid wearing them. We use the ironing board as a shelf for storage. You can find crumpled up clothes and soda cans just resting on our ironing board!

Cleaning the kitchen?

I clean the kitchen maybe twice a week, but nothing too intense. I definitely wouldn't consider it deep cleaning! Meghan will help occasionally if she was in there making guacamole or some other kind of snack, and feels like cleaning up.

The fridge can get pretty bad because nobody in the house takes the initiative to clean it. As long as the food doesn't go so bad that it starts to grow mold and move around on its own, we don't care what the condition of the fridge may be.

Other?

If the floors ever get washed around here, it's once a month at best. I just can't get down on my hands and knees anymore, so it goes undone unless John sees a mess and helps out.

It takes a lot of garbage or dishes to pile up before some one takes the initiative around here. Our theory is, "If you can stick your mess on the pile without anything falling off, you're good!"

When I run out of plates and cups downstairs I yell at the kids to go through their rooms and bring down all the dishes so I can wash them and put them back in the cupboard so we have something to eat with. If I didn't do that, we would all be eating with our hands!

PETS

How many pets do you have and what do they require?

I take care of the three cats in our home. They eat hard food and water. Two times a day they are given little snack packets of tuna meal or chicken meal.

SHOPPING

Who does the grocery shopping?

I do the shopping at the grocery store but the girls come with me because I like the company, and they are the only ones up before noon. I think the real reason they like to come shopping for groceries is so that when I'm not looking they can throw whatever crap they want into the shopping cart. They know I never put up a fuss because by the time we get to the cash register and pay I'm too exhausted to make them put everything back.

How often?

We end up going to the grocery store twice a week. We go through food quick so we have to go twice a week so we don't run out of everything we like to eat. We are always buying soda pop, toilet paper, and garbage bags.

I have spent up to 250 dollars a week on sodas, chips, dips, doughnuts, frozen pizzas and snacks for the house. It costs a lot of money to feed my family and all of the kids in the neighborhood!

Who chooses what is bought?

I shop for the basics every week. However, when I'm not looking, the girls put whatever they want into the cart. Half the time, I don't even know what I'm buying until I get to the cash register and have to pay for it all.

WEEKDAY MORNING ROUTINE

What time do you get up?

I've always been an early bird, so I normally wake up around 5:30 in the morning to start the day and play on my computer for about an hour. It gives me a little time by myself to relax before I have to start thinking about going to work or running my daily errands.

What time does everyone else get out of bed?

John gets up anywhere from 9:00 to 11:00 in the morning, takes a shower and putzs around the house playing pool in the basement and listening to his stereo before leaving for work. I wake the girls up around noon and we go out for breakfast or do something fun like go to the beach or the neighborhood pool. The boys wake when they feel like it, they are usually up by 3:00 in the afternoon at the latest.

Are you 'morning people?'

I consider myself a morning person surrounded by night owls because I am the only person who is up by what most people consider a decent hour.

What is the morning routine in your house?

I wake up around 5:30 in the morning and get in the shower by 6:30. By 8:00 in the morning I like to be out of the house so I can run my errands which are going to the bank, refilling on groceries if we've had a few people over the night before, or just going shopping. John is around the house getting ready for work. The house stays pretty quiet until about noon when I wake the girls up.

Who prepares breakfast? Does the family eat it together?

Sometimes breakfast happens so late that it turns into lunch. We go out 3 to 4 times a week for breakfast at a restaurant in our neighborhood. If we wait long enough Paul will make the cheesy eggs that Samantha taught him how to make or he'll make his famous pancakes.

What time do the kids leave for school?

Meghan leaves at 8:30 in the morning. She never makes it to the bus, even though the bus stops right in front of our house. Sometimes John yells to her that the bus is coming, just to see her run around and go crazy. Whoever has time in the morning will drive her to school, and we end up getting her there around 9:00 AM.

As far as schooling goes for the rest of the kids, Paul and Hector have chosen not to go to college, and are currently trying to figure out their next move. This doesn't worry us, because we know that the kids will figure out their lives for themselves. Samantha is enrolled at a local college and is currently on summer break.

Do you ever get to sleep in?

I don't like to sleep in. Sleeping in is for the kids. They have the rest of their lives to wake up early.

DAYTIME

What is your schedule for the day?

Once we get back from breakfast, around noon, the girls and I will come back home and see what the boys are doing. If the girls and I are having fun, we'll skip coming back home to check up on the boys and go ahead and get manicures and pedicures. I love getting my pedicures! Occasionally, Meghan and I also will get our hair done by Samantha here at the house. She cuts Paul and Hector's hair too. Even though Samantha doesn't work in a salon, she went to beauty school, so she knows what she's doing.

By 3:00 in the afternoon, the boys have gotten up and are either out fishing or upstairs in Paul's room working on his rap music.

Around 5:00 PM I will ask the kids what they want for dinner, and if they aren't hungry I will go and play on the computer again.

At 6:00 PM I get something to eat for myself. I will hang out in my room if there is something good on TV or hang out with the kids if they have friends over that are visiting and want to chat.

By 10:00PM I am in bed unless I am still visiting with the kids. I will continue to hang out with them all for a little bit and then go to my room.

What time do the kids finish school and how do they get home?

In the fall, Meghan usually gets out of school by 3:00 and I pick her up after work and bring her home.

Do they have any extra classes or activities after school? Who takes them and picks them up?

Meghan is not involved in any after school activities. Most of Meghan's friends are out of school.

When do the kids do their homework? Do you or your partner help them?

When Meghan does have homework, she does it at school in study hall. She never brings home her homework and she doesn't have any set times that she studies at home.. She's getting ready to repeat her senior year with junior credits because she didn't take her classes seriously her freshman year.

We're not involved with Meghan's homework on a daily basis, so we leave it up to her to get her assignments done. Her grades really don't bother us unless we get poor progress reports that say she is missing assignments. As long as she's trying, that's all that matters. There's more to life than good grades.

EVENING

If you work outside the home, what time do you get home from work?

I get home at 4:30 in the afternoon from work. John gets in around 11:30 at night.

What time is dinner? Who cooks it?

There is no such thing as a "set" dinner time in this house because we are a laid back household without a schedule. If you need to eat, just eat. There's no waiting on anyone around here. It been this way for so long that when John comes home from work, he knows to check the fridge for leftovers or eat a bag of chips or doughnuts for dinner.

What is your dinner routine?

There's no dinner routine! We're spontaneous. If we are all home, we'll sit around and chat about what everyone wants to eat. If everyone is busy doing their own thing, then they will feed themselves with leftovers, go through a drive thru, or find a snack to tide them over.

Who cleans up after dinner?

Nobody cleans up after dinner. I let the dishes sit until the next day and then I eventually get around to cleaning them.

What happens after dinner?

Everyone runs away from the mess in the kitchen and does their own their own thing. Usually the kids go up to their rooms. Occasionally, we'll chat in the living room or at the dining room table but that doesn't always happen.

Are your kids allowed out during the week? If so do they have a curfew?

The kids are allowed to do whatever they want during the week, but most of the time everyone comes over here. You can find kids anywhere in this house.

When my Paul goes out, I don't always know where he is. If he leaves when I'm not here, I have no clue where he's run off because we aren't the type of family that leaves notes letting everyone know where they are going. I always yell at him for it. I usually know where Meghan is because she calls me. Even if our kids don't tell us, we have a pretty good idea of where they start off their nights, but after that, we have no idea where they'll end up.

Do your kids have set bedtimes?

No. My kids are old enough to go to bed when they feel like it. Like I always say, "When you're tired, sleep."

What is the bedtime routine with the kids?

I am asleep when the kids go to bed. Sometimes they don't come in from fishing or hanging out with friends until 5:00 in the morning and I'm too old to be waiting up for them.

When I have seen them go to bed they start to wind down by playing video games and falling asleep with the TV on in their rooms or on the couches upstairs after they watched a movie or something.

What else do you do in the evening before you go to bed?

I like to play solitaire on the computer or watch TV because it relaxes me. John will come in from work and watch his favorite channels. He watches anything from military stuff to cartoons.

What time do you go to bed?

I get in bed around 10 at night unless the kids have friends over and I'm hanging out and chatting with them. Dad will get in bed anytime between midnight and 2 in the morning. I'm usually asleep by the time he gets into bed.

WEEKENDS

What does the family do on Saturday?

We get together and decide what to do for the day. We love to be spontaneous. We'll pick up and drive to another state if we feel like it. Dad only has off from work one Saturday a month so we try to do something together. Either we go to the beach, the Rockford speedway, or throw a party! It's fun, cheap, and loud and that's what we consider good family entertainment.

What's your Sunday morning routine?

It's the same as every day, there's nothing special about Sunday in this house. You won't see us in church, because we don't go. We believe God can hear you pray at home just as easy as he can at church.

What's your Sunday afternoon routine?

The kids do their own thing and so do we. I might do a project like clean a closet but that only happens once every few months.

What do you do Sunday evening?

If the kids are home, they may have friends over. Or we might rent a movie and watch it together. The kids always pick real bloody, scary movies - they love them! They scare me and I end up lying in bed worrying about who's going to jump out and get me!

THE RELATIONSHIP

How would you describe your relationship with your partner?

We're close and we talk but we are not "lovey-dovey" and that's okay with us. Put it this way, we're not dating. We're not holding hands constantly. We love each other and we don't have to say it.

What is the best thing about your relationship?

We are incredibly open with each other. We can sense how the other one feels. We just know and we don't even have to say it. We've been together since 1980 and have been married for 24 years.

What annoys you about your partner?

John can be anal about things, especially when it comes to who is parking in the driveway. I annoy John with my constant need to ask questions and get information. I have a sixth sense when something is going on.

What do your partner and you disagree about the most?

We rarely disagree. We don't keep our feelings inside, so that helps.

What happens when you disagree?

If we disagree I normally win! Chances are, if John

doesn't want me to do something, he knows I'll do it anyway. He doesn't put up a fight because he knows that he married a bull-headed woman. We just get over it and get on with things.

Do you disagree in front of the children?

We rarely disagree, but if we do it always happen in front of the children. It's part of having an open household.

FINANCES

Are you spenders or savers?

We spend it as fast as we get it! If we are ever short, we borrow from family. We would do the same if we could, because that's what family is for. We wish we were savers sometimes, but it's more important to enjoy life, have fun, and make people happy!

Who controls the money?

I control the money and I dole it out. John hates it when I forget to leave him money for work! Everyone is constantly coming up to me during the day and asking for a few dollars to do this and a few dollars to do that. Five bucks here and there for cigarettes and gas for the car adds up! When the money is gone, it's gone. But we enjoy it while we have it.

How much allowance do the children receive per week? Do they have to earn their allowance?

Whatever the kids ask for, we provide. They don't earn their money. If they had to earn it, they wouldn't get it.

How much do you spend on food & household items per week?

We spend about 300 dollars a week on food. Household items usually cost us around 100 dollars.

How much do you each spend on treats or vices per week?

We spend 150 a week on treats and vices and that goes mostly towards cigarettes for everyone.

If you need more money than that to live on, we suggest you get a Gold Card!

ANYTHING ELSE YOU WANT TO TELL ABOUT YOUR HOUSEHOLD?

It's important to remember your sense of humor around here! Remember that "You don't stop laughing because you grow old, you grow old because you stop laughing"! We're not meek, little mousy people. You always know how everyone feels around here because we are not afraid to tell you! We're not perfect. We never claim to be perfect. But we're who we are, and proud of it!

BOOKS BY EILEEN ORMSBY

Thank you for reading. I hope you found it informative and interesting. If you did, it would help s much if you were to take a minute to rate and review this book wherever you bought it, as this makes my books more visible to potential customers.

The following pages provide links and blurbs for my other books .

BOOKS BY EILEEN ORMSBY

A Manual for Murder: FREE AND EXCLUSIVE

Psycho.com: serial killers on the internet

Murder on the Dark Web: true stories from the dark side of the internet

Stalkers: true tales of deadly obsessions

Little Girls Lost: true tales of heinous crimes

Mishap or Murder? True tales of mysterious deaths and disappearances

The Darkest Web

Silk Road

Keep going for sneak peeks of these books and to find out how to get your FREE TRUE CRIME BOOK

A MANUAL FOR MURDER

THE TRUE STORY OF HOW A BOOK LED TO A TRIPLE HOMICIDE

When officers attend a triple homicide in a well-to-do neighborhood in Maryland, it looks like a robbery gone wrong. But why did the intruder kill a profoundly disabled boy who had no way of identifying him?

When the FBI is called in, their investigations take them from the glamorous world of Hollywood music royalty to the seediest districts of Detroit. It looks like the killer might have been too smart for them, until they find a book in a suspect's apartment, which may be the key to unraveling it all.

GET THIS EXCLUSIVE EBOOK AT EILEENORMSBY.COM

This book is not for sale and is only available to those who sign up for my newsletter. But don't worry: I won't spam you or pass your information on to anyone else. You can unsubscribe any time you like, even right after you download your free book! I don't mind, though I do hope you will stick around for updates to the cases I write about and to be first to know about any new books

LITTLE GIRLS LOST
TRUE TALES OF HEINOUS CRIMES

Four shocking crimes. Four lives lost. Countless lives shattered.

True stories of young lives cut brutally short that will make you want to hug your daughter and never let her go.

⚠ **Note: this is a true crime book that contains descriptions of sexual violence against children. Reader discretion is advised**

An 11-year-old girl never makes it home from a Halloween party. When the people of the tight-knit Oil City discover what was done to her, they cancel Halloween until the real monsters who roam their streets can be caught.

A 14-year-old girl is excited to attend her first evening party with local teens. What happens there is every parent's nightmare, but it is made infinitely worse when the residents of the town close ranks around the perpetrators.

A schoolgirl comes to the aid of a middle-aged woman who has lost her puppy and becomes the victim of the most hated couple in Australian history.

Police tell gang members a 16-year-old girl has agreed to testify against them, with predictable results. When they make an arrest for her murder, a Hollywood sitcom plays a surprising role in the outcome

HEAD TO EILEENORMSBY.COM FOR BUYING OPTIONS

STALKERS
TRUE TALES OF DEADLY OBSESSIONS

Deluded narcissists. Obsessed fans. Sinister internet trolls. Stalkers who turned deadly

A Hollywood starlet on a smash-hit sitcom enjoys rising fame, unaware that her greatest fan is hell-bent on meeting his crush. When she films a love scene, his adoration turns into a quest to see her punished

A gameshow winner turns to writing books. When one is given a scathing review, he tracks down the reviewer with bloody results

A teenage boy enjoys online chatrooms. When he meets a sexy Secret Service operative, she convinces him he has been chosen to be a spy with a licence to kill... and his first target is his own best friend.

Men keep turning up at a newlywed's home convinced that she has placed a Craigslist ad for a rough fantasy roleplay. Things turn violent before police are able to unravel a twisted and diabolical scheme

STALKERS takes you into the twisted world of cyberstalking, catfishing, rejected suitors, jealous exes and celebrity stalkers, and the devastating impact their obsessions can have on their victims. This is a standalone book in the Dark Webs True Crime series. It is not necessary to have read the others in the series

HEAD TO EILEENORMSBY.COM FOR BUYING OPTIONS

PSYCHO.COM
SERIAL KILLERS ON THE INTERNET

True tales of serial killers who went viral

Serial killers have been with us for decades. The internet has put them in our pockets

The Dnepropetrovsk Maniacs: A pair of teens go on a murderous spree, filming themselves along the way. When their deadly rampage is finished, more than 20 are dead and their exploits are immortalized in the most shocking video ever to circulate the internet, "**3 Guys, 1 Hammer**"

Pedro Rodrigues Filho, aka "Killer Petey": A serial killer with over 100 kills to his name prides himself on killing only murderers, rapists and pedophiles. When he walks free, he becomes a Youtube sensation

Mark Twitchell, aka the "Dexter" Serial Killer: A psychopath lures victims through online dating to use as "research" for his twisted film project

Psycho.com is a chilling look at what happens when murderous minds meet modern technology.

"What I loved most about the book is it wasn't just about the killers and what made them tick, but also focused on the victims who deserved to be remembered just as much if not more" - reviewer

HEAD TO EILEENORMSBY.COM FOR BUYING OPTIONS

MURDER ON THE DARK WEB

TRUE STORIES FROM THE DARK SIDE OF THE INTERNET

A look into the dark side of the internet's secret underbelly

A Minnesota dog trainer is found dead of an apparent suicide after detectives find her details on a dark web murder-for-hire site. But who paid $13,000 in Bitcoin to kill this devout Christian and beloved wife and mother?

An Instagram glamour model is drugged, kidnapped and listed for sale on a dark web human trafficking site. A secret society called Black Death demands a ransom for her safe return, or else she will be sold to sadistic millionaires to use before feeding to the tigers.

The dark web is the internet's evil twin, where anything can be bought and sold. Drugs, weapons, and hackers-for-hire are available at the touch of a button.

Most who visit merely look around, happy to simply satisfy their curiosity before leaving, never to return. But some are sucked into the criminal underworld and find themselves doing things they would never have contemplated in the real world—ordering a hit on a love rival or bidding on an auction for a sex slave—like the people in this book.

These are extraordinary true tales of infidelity, betrayal and shadowy hitmen and human traffickers who may not be that they seem.

HEAD TO EILEENORMSBY.COM FOR BUYING OPTIONS

MISHAP OR MURDER?

TRUE TALES OF MYSTERIOUS DEATHS AND DISAPPEARANCES

It takes just seconds for someone to die. But sometimes years later, questions remain: was it an accident, suicide, or something far more sinister?

An elderly couple having an illicit affair disappear into the bush, their campsite destroyed by fire but their vehicle untouched. At first police wonder if they got lost or eloped, but their investigation soon turns to homicide. Who are the mysterious "Hill People" and does a missing drone hold the key to the mystery?

A skydiver plunges to his death and investigators soon discover his parachute had been tampered with. But with a hundred potential murder weapons and just as many suspects who are used to the adrenaline rush of a high-stakes sport, can anyone uncover who did it?

A young mother heads out for a night on the town to celebrate her new car and never comes home. Her text messages and car tracking system tell a story right up to the moment she disappears, leaving police baffled. Did she disconnect the GPS herself or was someone in the car with her that night?

An entire town is wary of a hard-living local man, and none more so than his battered wife. When he disappears and she starts selling his possessions, nobody cares enough to interfere, until his sister starts asking questions. Did he really leave his wife and four children, or do the local mineshafts hold more secrets than gold?

The latest in the Dark Webs True Crime series takes you through these stories and more cases that stumped police and investigators for years.

Was it Mishap... or Murder?

THE DARKEST WEB

The Darkest Web

Dark...

A kingpin willing to murder to protect his dark web drug empire. A corrupt government official determined to avoid exposure. The death of a dark web drugs czar in mysterious circumstances in a Bangkok jail cell, just as the author arrives there.

Who is Variety Jones and why have darknet markets ballooned tenfold since authorities shut down the original dark web drugs bazaar, Silk Road? Who are the kingpins willing to sell poisons and weapons, identities and bank accounts, malware and life-ruining services online to anyone with a wallet full of Bitcoin?

Darker...

A death in Minnesota leads detectives into the world of dark web murder-for-hire where hundreds of thousands of dollars in Bitcoin is paid to arrange killings, beatings and rapes. Meanwhile, the owner of the most successful hitman website in history is threatening the journalists who investigate his business with a visit from his operatives - and the author is at the top of his list.

Darkest...

People with the most depraved perversions gather to share their obscene materials in an almost inaccessible corner of the dark web. A video circulates and the pursuit of the monsters responsible for 'Daisy's Destruction' lead detectives into the unimaginable horror of the world of hurtcore.

There's the world wide web - the internet we all know that connects us via news, email, forums, shopping and social media. Then there's the dark web - the parallel internet accessed by only a select few. Usually, those it connects wish to remain anonymous and for good reason.

Eileen Ormsby has spent the past five years exploring every corner of the Dark Web. She has shopped on darknet markets, contributed to forums, waited in red rooms and been threatened by hitmen on murder-for-hire sites. On occasions, her dark web activities have poured out into the real world and she has attended trials, met with criminals and the law enforcement who tracked them down, interviewed dark web identities and visited them in prison.

This book will take you into the murkiest depths of the web's dark underbelly: a place of hitmen for hire, red rooms, hurtcore sites and markets that will sell anything a person is willing to pay for - including another person. The Darkest Web.

Published by Allen & Unwin

HEAD TO EILEENORMSBY.COM FOR BUYING OPTIONS

SILK ROAD

It was the 'eBay of drugs', a billion dollar empire. Behind it was the FBI's Most Wanted Man, a mysterious crime czar dubbed 'Dread Pirate Roberts'. SILK ROAD lay at the heart of the 'Dark Web' - a parallel internet of porn, guns, assassins and drugs. Lots of drugs. With the click of a button LSD, heroin, meth, coke, any illegal drug imaginable, would wing its way by regular post from any dealer to any user in the world. How was this online drug cartel even possible? And who was the mastermind all its low roads led to? This is the incredible true story of Silk Road's rise and fall, told with unparalleled insight into the main players - including alleged founder and kingpin Dread Pirate Roberts himself - by lawyer and investigative journalist Eileen Ormsby. A stunning crime story with a truth that explodes off the page.

Published by Pan MacMillan

HEAD TO EILEENORMSBY.COM FOR BUYING OPTIONS

FROM THE AUTHOR

Thank you for giving me your valuable time to share these stories with you.

A great deal of work goes into researching these crimes and writing about them in a way that gives voice to the victims. The most important part of how well a book sells is how many positive reviews it has, so if you leave me one then you are directly helping me to continue to report on these stories for you.

Just a line or two is all it takes to make an author's day.

SEARCH FOR "SMALL TOWNS, DARK SECRETS" ON AMAZON OR GOODREADS TO LEAVE YOUR REVIEW

Thank you so much.

Made in United States
Troutdale, OR
01/27/2024

17230201R00186